Robert J. Marzano

Debra J. Pickering

Jane E. Pollock

Classroom Instruction *that* works

RESEARCH-
BASED STRATEGIES
FOR INCREASING STUDENT ACHIEVEMENT

PEARSON

Merrill
Prentice Hall

Upper Saddle River, New Jersey
Columbus, Ohio

Library of Congress Cataloging-in-Publication Data

Marzano, Robert J.

   Classroom instruction that works : research-based strategies for increasing student achievement / Robert J. Marzano, Debra J. Pickering, Jane E. Pollock.

     p. cm.

Includes bibliographical references (p.   ) and index.

"ASCD product no. 100043"—T.p. verso.

ISBN 0-87120-504-1

   1. Effective teaching—United States.   2. Academic achievement—United States—Statistics.   I. Pickering, Debra.   II. Pollock, Jane E., 1956–   III. Title

     LB1025.3 .M339 2001

     371.102—dc21

                                    00-012007

This special edition published by Merrill Education/Prentice Hall, Inc. by arrangement with the Association for Supervision and Curriculum Development.

Vice President and Publisher: Jeffery W. Johnston
Executive Editor: Kevin M. Davis
Director of Marketing: Ann Davis
Marketing Manager: Autumn Purdy
Marketing Coordinator: Barbara Koontz

This book was printed and bound by Courier/Kendallville. The cover was printed by Phoenix Color Corporation.

21 22 23 24 25
ISBN: 0-13-119503-4

Classroom Instruction that works

Research-Based Strategies for Increasing Student Achievement

LIST OF FIGURES

confidence in the findings of educational research was addressed in depth in 1987 in an article by researcher Larry Hedges entitled "How Hard Is Hard Science: How Soft Is Soft Science?" Hedges examined studies across 13 areas of research in psychology and education, which he referred to as the "social sciences," and compared them with studies in physics. He found that the studies from physics were almost identical to the studies from the social sciences in terms of their variability: "Almost 50% of the reviews showed statistically significant disagreements in both the social sciences and the physical sciences" (p. 450). Thus, studies in physics exhibit the same discrepancies in results as do studies in education—one study shows that a particular technique works; the next study shows that it does not. Hedges also found that researchers in the hard sciences much more frequently discard studies that seemed to report "extreme findings." For example, in the area of particle physics, roughly 40 percent of the studies were omitted from a synthesis of studies because their findings were considered unexplainable. However, in education and psychology, Hedges found that it is rare for even 10 percent of studies with extreme findings to be discarded when research is synthesized.

Hedges' overall conclusion was that research in the soft sciences like education is, indeed, comparable to research in the hard sciences in terms of its rigor. Hedges' overall recommendation was that educators,

like researchers in the hard sciences, look for general trends in the findings from studies. In other words, findings from no single study or even a small set of studies should be taken as the final word on whether a strategy or approach works well. Instead, as many studies as can be found on a given topic should be analyzed. The composite results of those findings should be considered the best estimate of what is known about that topic.

Overall Effects of Instructional Techniques

To prepare this book, researchers at Mid-continent Research for Education and Learning (McREL) analyzed selected research studies on instructional strategies that could be used by teachers in K–12 classrooms (see Marzano, 1998, for a more detailed description of that effort). We used a research technique referred to as *meta-analysis*. A meta-analysis combines the results from a number of studies to determine the average effect of a given technique. When conducting a meta-analysis, a researcher translates the results of a given study into a unit of measurement referred to as an *effect size*. An effect size expresses the increase or decrease in achievement of the experimental group (the group of students who are exposed to a specific instructional technique) in standard deviation units. To illustrate, assume that the effect

1

APPLYING THE RESEARCH ON INSTRUCTION: AN IDEA WHOSE TIME HAS COME

We educators stand at a special point in time. This is not because a new decade, century, and millennium have begun (although this phenomenon certainly brings new opportunities and complexities). Rather, it is because the "art" of teaching is rapidly becoming the "science" of teaching, and this is a relatively new phenomenon. It may come as a surprise to some readers that up until about 30 years ago, teaching had not been systematically studied in a scientific manner. This is not to say that effective teaching strategies were absent before 1970. Indeed, educators have effectively used Socratic inquiry as an explicit instructional strategy for two and one half millennia. At the beginning of the 1970s, however, researchers began to look at the effects of instruction on student learning. In fact, the decade before was marked by the belief that school really made little difference in the achievement

of students. This was a conclusion of the now famous report entitled *Equality of Educational Opportunity* published in 1966 (see Coleman et al., 1966). The report is commonly referred to as the "Coleman report" in deference to its senior author, James Coleman. After analyzing data from some 600,000 students and 60,000 teachers in more than 4,000 schools, Coleman and his colleagues concluded that the quality of schooling a student receives accounts for only about 10 percent of the variance in student achievement.

To understand what this means, consider the following example: Assume you are analyzing the science achievement scores for a group of 100 eighth-grade students from three different schools. These students will no doubt vary greatly in their science achievement. Some will have very low scores, some very high scores, and some in the middle. The findings from the

Coleman report indicate that only 10 percent of these differences are caused by the quality of the schools these 100 students attend. In other words, going to the best of the three schools as opposed to the worst of the three schools, will change only about 10 percent of the differences in student achievement.

A logical question is, What influences the other 90 percent? Coleman and his colleagues concluded that the vast majority of differences in student achievement can be attributed to factors like the student's natural ability or aptitude, the socioeconomic status of the student, and the student's home environment. Unfortunately, these are all things that cannot be changed by schools. These same findings were corroborated by Harvard researcher Christopher Jencks in his book *Inequality: A Reassessment of the Effects of Family and Schools in America* (see Jencks et al., 1972). Jencks and his colleagues re-analyzed much of the data used in the Coleman report. Again, the conclusion that schools make little difference was pre-eminent. As Jencks notes: "Most differences in . . . test scores are due to factors that schools do not control" (p. 109).

The conclusions by Coleman and Jencks did not paint a very hopeful picture for educators and education. If most of what influences student achievement is out of the control of schools, why even try? Fortunately, in retrospect, we now see some serious flaws in these conclusions. In fact,

we now can look at the possible influence of schools and teachers with great hope. But how is this so? First, the technique used by Coleman and Jencks of focusing on the percentage of explained differences in scores paints an unnecessarily gloomy picture. This point has been made quite eloquently and convincingly by researcher Robert Rosenthal and by researchers John Hunter and Frank Schmidt. Those interested in a technical discussion should consult Rosenthal (1991) and Hunter and Schmidt (1990). Briefly, though, the more meaningful way to interpret the Coleman and Jencks finding is in terms of percentile gain in achievement. (We will explain this in more depth in a subsequent section.) To illustrate, the finding that schools account for only 10 percent of the differences in student achievement translates into a percentile gain of about 23 points. That is, the average student who attends a "good" school will have a score that is 23 percentile points higher than the average student who attends a poor school. From this perspective, schools definitely can make a difference in student achievement.

The second and more important reason that we now have a more optimistic view of what schools can do, is that research conducted since the Coleman and Jencks studies has shown that an individual teacher can have a powerful effect on her students *even if the school doesn't*. This finding makes the most sense if we remember that Coleman and Jencks examined the

average effect of schools. Within a given school, though, there is a great deal of variation in the quality of instruction from teacher to teacher. If we can identify what those highly effective teachers do, then even more of the differences in student achievement can be accounted for.

The conclusion that individual teachers can have a profound influence on student learning even in schools that are relatively ineffective, was first noticed in the 1970s when we began to examine effective teaching practices. In fact, after reviewing hundreds of studies conducted in the 1970s, researchers Jere Brophy and Thomas Good (1986) commented: "The myth that teachers do not make a difference in student learning has been refuted" (p. 370).

More recently, researcher William Sanders and his colleagues (see Sanders & Horn, 1994; Wright, Horn, & Sanders, 1997) have noted that the individual classroom teacher has even more of an effect on student achievement than originally thought. As a result of analyzing the achievement scores of more than 100,000 students across hundreds of schools, their conclusion was

> The results of this study will document that the most important factor affecting student learning is the teacher. In addition, the results show wide variation in effectiveness among teachers. The immediate and clear implication of this finding is that seemingly more can be done to improve education by improving the effectiveness of teachers than by any other single factor. *Effective teachers appear to be effective with students of all achievement levels, regardless of the level of heterogeneity in their classrooms.* If the teacher is ineffective, students under the teacher's tutelage will show inadequate progress academically regardless of how similar or different they are regarding their academic achievement (Wright et al., 1997, p. 63).

This book attempts to add practical perspectives to the optimistic picture presented by the research conducted since the works of Coleman and Jencks. This book presents and exemplifies instructional strategies that we have extracted from the research base on effective instruction. Teachers can use these strategies to guide classroom practice in such a way as to maximize the possibility of enhancing student achievement. Before presenting these strategies, however, we first briefly consider the nature and quality of educational research in general.

Attitudes About Educational Research

Although a great deal of educational research has been and is currently being conducted in many universities and research centers, some educators and noneducators hold a fairly low opinion of that research. Some people believe that research in education is not as rigorous or conclusive as research in the "hard sciences," such as physics and chemistry. The general lack

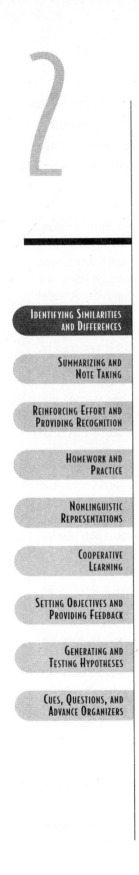

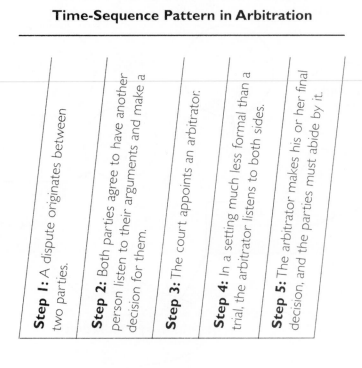

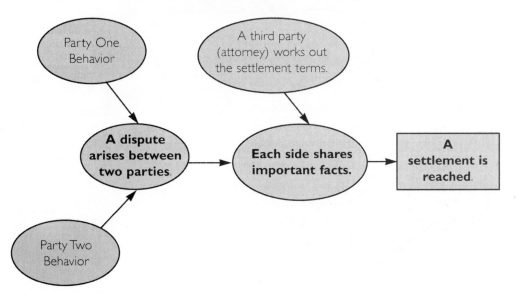

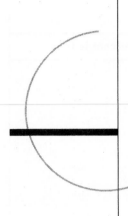

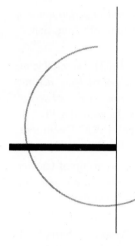

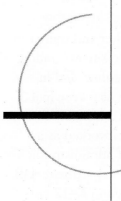

1

Applying the Research on Instruction: An Idea Whose Time Has Come

We educators stand at a special point in time. This is not because a new decade, century, and millennium have begun (although this phenomenon certainly brings new opportunities and complexities). Rather, it is because the "art" of teaching is rapidly becoming the "science" of teaching, and this is a relatively new phenomenon. It may come as a surprise to some readers that up until about 30 years ago, teaching had not been systematically studied in a scientific manner. This is not to say that effective teaching strategies were absent before 1970. Indeed, educators have effectively used Socratic inquiry as an explicit instructional strategy for two and one half millennia. At the beginning of the 1970s, however, researchers began to look at the effects of instruction on student learning. In fact, the decade before was marked by the belief that school really made little difference in the achievement of students. This was a conclusion of the now famous report entitled *Equality of Educational Opportunity* published in 1966 (see Coleman et al., 1966). The report is commonly referred to as the "Coleman report" in deference to its senior author, James Coleman. After analyzing data from some 600,000 students and 60,000 teachers in more than 4,000 schools, Coleman and his colleagues concluded that the quality of schooling a student receives accounts for only about 10 percent of the variance in student achievement.

To understand what this means, consider the following example: Assume you are analyzing the science achievement scores for a group of 100 eighth-grade students from three different schools. These students will no doubt vary greatly in their science achievement. Some will have very low scores, some very high scores, and some in the middle. The findings from the

Coleman report indicate that only 10 percent of these differences are caused by the quality of the schools these 100 students attend. In other words, going to the best of the three schools as opposed to the worst of the three schools, will change only about 10 percent of the differences in student achievement.

A logical question is, What influences the other 90 percent? Coleman and his colleagues concluded that the vast majority of differences in student achievement can be attributed to factors like the student's natural ability or aptitude, the socioeconomic status of the student, and the student's home environment. Unfortunately, these are all things that cannot be changed by schools. These same findings were corroborated by Harvard researcher Christopher Jencks in his book *Inequality: A Reassessment of the Effects of Family and Schools in America* (see Jencks et al., 1972). Jencks and his colleagues re-analyzed much of the data used in the Coleman report. Again, the conclusion that schools make little difference was pre-eminent. As Jencks notes: "Most differences in . . . test scores are due to factors that schools do not control" (p. 109).

The conclusions by Coleman and Jencks did not paint a very hopeful picture for educators and education. If most of what influences student achievement is out of the control of schools, why even try? Fortunately, in retrospect, we now see some serious flaws in these conclusions. In fact,

we now can look at the possible influence of schools and teachers with great hope. But how is this so? First, the technique used by Coleman and Jencks of focusing on the percentage of explained differences in scores paints an unnecessarily gloomy picture. This point has been made quite eloquently and convincingly by researcher Robert Rosenthal and by researchers John Hunter and Frank Schmidt. Those interested in a technical discussion should consult Rosenthal (1991) and Hunter and Schmidt (1990). Briefly, though, the more meaningful way to interpret the Coleman and Jencks finding is in terms of percentile gain in achievement. (We will explain this in more depth in a subsequent section.) To illustrate, the finding that schools account for only 10 percent of the differences in student achievement translates into a percentile gain of about 23 points. That is, the average student who attends a "good" school will have a score that is 23 percentile points higher than the average student who attends a poor school. From this perspective, schools definitely can make a difference in student achievement.

The second and more important reason that we now have a more optimistic view of what schools can do, is that research conducted since the Coleman and Jencks studies has shown that an individual teacher can have a powerful effect on her students *even if the school doesn't*. This finding makes the most sense if we remember that Coleman and Jencks examined the

average effect of schools. Within a given school, though, there is a great deal of variation in the quality of instruction from teacher to teacher. If we can identify what those highly effective teachers do, then even more of the differences in student achievement can be accounted for.

The conclusion that individual teachers can have a profound influence on student learning even in schools that are relatively ineffective, was first noticed in the 1970s when we began to examine effective teaching practices. In fact, after reviewing hundreds of studies conducted in the 1970s, researchers Jere Brophy and Thomas Good (1986) commented: "The myth that teachers do not make a difference in student learning has been refuted" (p. 370).

More recently, researcher William Sanders and his colleagues (see Sanders & Horn, 1994; Wright, Horn, & Sanders, 1997) have noted that the individual classroom teacher has even more of an effect on student achievement than originally thought. As a result of analyzing the achievement scores of more than 100,000 students across hundreds of schools, their conclusion was

> The results of this study will document that the most important factor affecting student learning is the teacher. In addition, the results show wide variation in effectiveness among teachers. The immediate and clear implication of this finding is that seemingly more can be done to improve education by improving the effectiveness of teachers than by any other single factor. *Effective teachers appear to be effective with students of all achievement levels, regardless of the level of heterogeneity in their classrooms.* If the teacher is ineffective, students under the teacher's tutelage will show inadequate progress academically regardless of how similar or different they are regarding their academic achievement (Wright et al., 1997, p. 63).

This book attempts to add practical perspectives to the optimistic picture presented by the research conducted since the works of Coleman and Jencks. This book presents and exemplifies instructional strategies that we have extracted from the research base on effective instruction. Teachers can use these strategies to guide classroom practice in such a way as to maximize the possibility of enhancing student achievement. Before presenting these strategies, however, we first briefly consider the nature and quality of educational research in general.

Attitudes About Educational Research

Although a great deal of educational research has been and is currently being conducted in many universities and research centers, some educators and noneducators hold a fairly low opinion of that research. Some people believe that research in education is not as rigorous or conclusive as research in the "hard sciences," such as physics and chemistry. The general lack of confidence in the findings of educational research was addressed in depth in 1987 in an article by researcher Larry Hedges entitled "How Hard Is Hard Science: How Soft Is Soft Science?" Hedges examined studies across 13 areas of research in psychology and education, which he referred to as the "social sciences," and compared them with studies in physics. He found that the studies from physics were almost identical to the studies from the social sciences in terms of their variability: "Almost 50% of the reviews showed statistically significant disagreements in both the social sciences and the physical sciences" (p. 450). Thus, studies in physics exhibit the same discrepancies in results as do studies in education—one study shows that a particular technique works; the next study shows that it does not. Hedges also found that researchers in the hard sciences much more frequently discard studies that seemed to report "extreme findings." For example, in the area of particle physics, roughly 40 percent of the studies were omitted from a synthesis of studies because their findings were considered unexplainable. However, in education and psychology, Hedges found that it is rare for even 10 percent of studies with extreme findings to be discarded when research is synthesized.

Hedges' overall conclusion was that research in the soft sciences like education is, indeed, comparable to research in the hard sciences in terms of its rigor. Hedges' overall recommendation was that educators, like researchers in the hard sciences, look for general trends in the findings from studies. In other words, findings from no single study or even a small set of studies should be taken as the final word on whether a strategy or approach works well. Instead, as many studies as can be found on a given topic should be analyzed. The composite results of those findings should be considered the best estimate of what is known about that topic.

Overall Effects of Instructional Techniques

To prepare this book, researchers at Mid-continent Research for Education and Learning (McREL) analyzed selected research studies on instructional strategies that could be used by teachers in K–12 classrooms (see Marzano, 1998, for a more detailed description of that effort). We used a research technique referred to as *meta-analysis*. A meta-analysis combines the results from a number of studies to determine the average effect of a given technique. When conducting a meta-analysis, a researcher translates the results of a given study into a unit of measurement referred to as an *effect size*. An effect size expresses the increase or decrease in achievement of the experimental group (the group of students who are exposed to a specific instructional technique) in standard deviation units. To illustrate, assume that the effect

FIGURE 1.1

The Normal Distribution

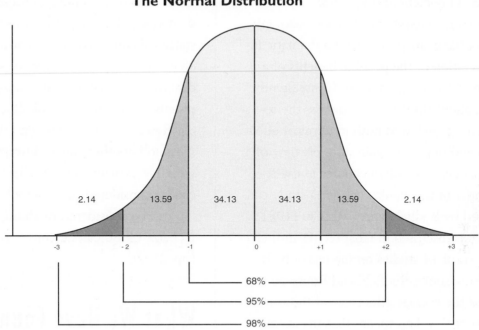

size computed for a specific study is 1.0. This means that the average score for students in the experimental group is 1.0 standard deviation higher than the average scores of students in the control group. Another way of saying this is that a student at the 50th percentile in the experimental group would be one standard deviation higher than a student at the 50th percentile in the control group.

One of the more useful aspects of an effect size is that it can be easily translated into a percentile gain—recall that we talked about percentile gains in the first section of this chapter. Here's how it is done. Statisticians inform us that, in general, we can expect students' achievement scores to be distributed like the well known "bell curve"

or "normal distribution." Figure 1.1 depicts the normal distribution.

Figure 1.1 shows that the normal distribution has a range of about three standard deviations above the mean and three standard deviations below the mean. Figure 1.1 also depicts the fact that about 34 percent of the scores in the normal distribution will be found in the interval between the mean and the first standard deviation above the mean, about 14 percent of the scores will be found in the interval between the first standard deviation and the second standard deviation, and so on. Going back to our example of the study that showed an effect size of 1.0 standard deviations, we can now interpret this in terms of percentile gain. An effect size of 1.0 means a percentile gain of 34 points—one standard deviation above the mean encompasses 34 percent of the scores.

Being able to translate effect sizes into percentile gains provides for a dramatic interpretation of the possible benefits of a given instructional strategy. Consequently, throughout this book, we discuss the research we reviewed both in terms of effect sizes and percentile gain. As a preview of discussions you will encounter in the remainder of this book, consider a study conducted by Redfield and Rousseau (1981), which is discussed in Chapter 10. In their analysis of 14 studies on the use of higher-level questions, Redfield and Rousseau computed the average effect size of those studies to be .73. This means that the average student who was exposed to higher-level questioning strategies scored 0.73 standard deviations above the scores of the average

student who was not exposed to higher-level questioning strategies (depicted by the shaded area in Figure 1.2). By consulting a statistical conversion table, for transforming effect sizes to percentile gains (see Appendix), we find that an effect size of 0.73 represents a percentile gain of about 27 points.

Researcher Jacob Cohen (1988) presents still another way of interpreting effect sizes. He explains that an effect size of .20 can be considered small; an effect size of .50 can be considered medium; and an effect size of .80 can be considered large (pp. 25–26).

What We Have Found

One of the primary goals of the McREL study was to identify those instructional

FIGURE 1.2

Average Effect Size Using Higher-Level Questions

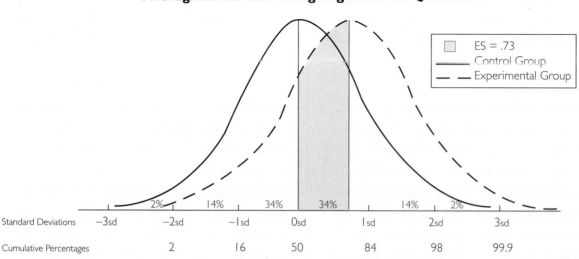

FIGURE 1.3
Categories of Instructional Strategies That Affect Student Achievement

Category	Ave. Effect Size (ES)	Percentile Gain	No. of ESs	Standard Deviation (SD)
Identifying similarities and differences	1.61	45	31	.31
Summarizing and note taking	1.00	34	179	.50
Reinforcing effort and providing recognition	.80	29	21	.35
Homework and practice	.77	28	134	.36
Nonlinguistic representations	.75	27	246	.40
Cooperative learning	.73	27	122	.40
Setting objectives and providing feedback	.61	23	408	.28
Generating and testing hypotheses	.61	23	63	.79
Questions, cues, and advance organizers	.59	22	1,251	.26

Note: We caution readers that it is impossible to derive the average effect sizes shown in this figure from the effect-size information provided in the figures in Chapters 2–10, which list the synthesis studies used in the analysis of the instructional strategy under discussion. The synthesis studies listed for a given category of instructional strategy often involve the review of some of the same research, and thus involve some of the same comparisons between experimental and control groups. An "average of these averages" would lead to inaccurate conclusions. The average effect sizes reported in Figure 1.3 are based on comparisons that are independent. Since these averages do not include overlapping data, they provide a more accurate summary statement about the effect of a particular category of instructional strategy.

strategies that have a high probability of enhancing student achievement for all students in all subject areas at all grade levels. Figure 1.3 lists nine categories of strategies that have a strong effect on student achievement.

Subsequent chapters of this book discuss these nine categories in depth. It is useful, however, to consider them as a group briefly. As indicated in Figure 1.3, the average effect sizes of these strategies range from 1.61 to .59. One of the most important things to remember when interpreting Figure 1.3 is that the effect sizes reported in the first column (Average Effect Sizes) are averages for the various studies we examined. Some of the studies had effect sizes much higher than the average; some had effect sizes much lower than the average. In fact, the expected range of effect sizes for a given category of instructional techniques is a spread of six standard deviations (three standard deviations above the average effect size and three standard deviations below the average effect size). To illustrate, consider the general category of instructional strategies referred to as *reinforcing effort and providing recognition*. As shown in Figure 1.3, the average effect size for this category is .80 and the standard deviation is .35. We also see that 21 studies were used to compute the average effect size of .80. The standard deviation of .35 tells us how different those 21 studies were. Among the 21 studies that were reviewed to compute the average effect size (.80), some had an effect size as high as three standard deviations above the mean—since the standard deviation is .35, three times .35 is 1.05. Therefore, some effect sizes in the set of 21 were as high as 1.85 (.80 + 1.05). Conversely, some effect sizes in the set of 21 were three standard deviations below the mean of .80. Thus, some effect sizes were as low as −.35 (.80 − 1.05). Some of the studies, then, have negative effect sizes. A negative effect size means that the experimental group actually performed *worse* than the control group.

The inference that should be drawn from this illustration is that no instructional strategy works equally well in all situations. We strongly recommend that you keep this in mind as you review the strategies presented in this book and apply them in classrooms. Instructional strategies are tools only. Although the strategies presented in this book are certainly good tools, they should not be expected to work equally well in all situations.

What You Will Find in This Book

Chapters 2–10 discuss the nine categories of instructional strategies and provide in-depth examples of each. Most of these chapters have the same format. First, we summarize the research and theory. Whenever possible, we present the findings of specific studies in effect size and percentile gain units related to the particular strategy. Next, we discuss generalizations about classroom practice. These generalizations might be considered guiding principles for use of the instructional strategies presented in each chapter. Finally, we describe explicit instructional strategies and present examples. Although busy practitioners might be tempted to skip directly to the specific instructional strategies, we strongly recommend that you read the research and theory syntheses for each section, along with the generalizations. A thorough understanding of both will provide a basis for a much more thoughtful analysis and use of the specific instructional strategies.

What We Don't Know Yet

Although our synthesis of the research has taught us a great deal, there are still many questions as yet unanswered by this research. Some of them are

◆ Are some instructional strategies more effective in certain subject areas?

◆ Are some instructional strategies more effective at certain grade levels?

◆ Are some instructional strategies more effective with students from different backgrounds?

◆ Are some instructional strategies more effective with students of different aptitude?

These are important questions, the answers to which will surely help move teaching from an art to a science. Until then, we should proceed with caution. In fact, the unexamined use of instructional strategies might produce some unintended negative outcomes. To illustrate, researchers Van Secker and Lissitz (1999) studied the effects on student science achievement of some instructional techniques that are recommended in the National Science Education Standard (National Research Council, 1996). These strategies were

◆ Student-centered instructions
◆ Teaching of critical thinking skills
◆ Use of "hands-on" laboratory activities

In general, all three of these strategies exhibited positive effects on the science achievement of 10th grade students. Specifically, the effect size for student-centered instruction was 1.07, the effect size for teaching of critical thinking was .12, and

the effect size for use of hands-on laboratory actually was .85. The researchers also found, however, that an emphasis on student-centered instruction actually increased the differences in science achievement between boys and girls and an emphasis on critical thinking actually increased the differences in achievement between minority and majority students and between students with high socioeconomic status (SES) and students with low SES. Although we should draw no hard and fast conclusions from the Van Secker and Lissitz study, it illustrates the need to study the effects of instructional strategies on specific types of students in specific situations, with specific subject matters. Until we find the answers to the preceding questions, teachers should rely on their knowledge of their students, their subject matter, and their situation to identify the most appropriate instructional strategies.

What We Have Not Included

We need to make one final comment on the limitations of the conclusions that educators can draw from reading this book. Although the title of this book speaks to instruction in a general sense, you should note that we have limited our focus to instructional strategies. There are certainly other aspects of classroom pedagogy that affect student achievement. In fact, we

FIGURE 1.4

Three Elements of Effective Pedagogy

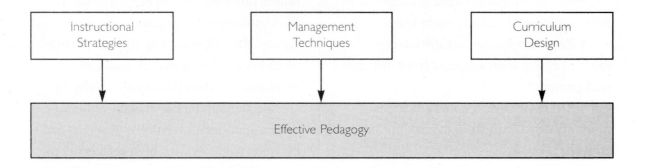

might postulate that effective pedagogy involves three related areas: (1) the instructional strategies used by the teacher, (2) the management techniques used by the teacher, and (3) the curriculum designed by the teacher (see Figure 1.4). This book addresses only the first element of the tripartite. McREL is attempting to synthesize the research in the other two areas.

With all of the limitations of this book acknowledged, we again affirm our belief that we are at the beginning of a new era in education—one in which research will provide strong, explicit guidance for the classroom teacher. We hope that this book will help usher in that new era.

Research-
Based
Strategies

2

IDENTIFYING SIMILARITIES AND DIFFERENCES

As part of their study of the decade of the 1960s, students in Mrs. Jackson's American History class read about and listened to Martin Luther King, Jr.'s speech, "I Have A Dream." Mrs. Jackson knew that these students had been exposed to this speech many times before and, therefore, was not surprised when they offered only predictable comments in the class discussion. In order to help students understand the speech in a different way and to build on the knowledge they had gained throughout the year, Mrs. Jackson presented the following incomplete analogy:

"I Have a Dream" was to the Civil Rights Movement as

_____ was to _____.

In small groups, students were to complete the analogy using another historical event or document in the first blank and a movement or event in the second blank. The students were asked to be ready to explain their completed analogy to the entire class.

To Mrs. Jackson's surprise, students were quite adept in designing and explaining their analogies. To the students' surprise, this activity deepened their understanding of the effect the "I Have a Dream" speech had on the Civil Rights Movement.

Mrs. Jackson has engaged her students in a complex and abstract form of identifying similarities and differences by having them generate and explain analogies.

Research and Theory on Identifying Similarities and Differences

This first general category of instructional strategies is entitled "identifying similarities and differences." Researchers have found these mental operations to be basic to human thought (see Gentner & Markman, 1994; Markman & Gentner, 1993a, 1993b; Medin, Goldstone, & Markman, 1995). Indeed, they might be considered the "core" of all learning.

The overall power of identifying similarities and differences is, perhaps, best illustrated by an experiment conducted by Gick and Holyoak (1980). They presented their subjects with the following problem (which was adapted from a study by Duncker, 1945):

> Suppose you are a doctor faced with a patient who has a malignant tumor in his stomach. It is impossible to operate on the patient, but unless the tumor is destroyed the patient will die. There is a kind of ray that can be used to destroy the tumor. If the rays reach the tumor all at once at a sufficiently high intensity, the healthy tissue that the rays pass through on the way to the tumor will also be destroyed. At lower intensities the rays are harmless to healthy tissue, but they will not affect the tumor either. What type of procedure might be used to destroy the tumor with the rays and, at the same time, avoid destroying the healthy tissue (pp. 307–308)?

In general, only 10 percent of people can solve this problem when first presented with it. Gick and Holyoak, however, also presented their subjects with the following story:

> A small country was ruled from a strong fortress by a dictator. The fortress was situated in the middle of the country, surrounded by farms and villages. Many roads led to the fortress through the countryside. A rebel general vowed to capture the fortress. The general knew that an attack by his entire army would capture the fortress. He gathered his army at the head of one of the roads, ready to launch a full-scale direct attack.
>
> However, the general then learned that the dictator had planted mines on each of the roads. The mines were set so that small bodies of men could pass over them safely, since the dictator needed to move his troops and workers to and from the fortress. However, any large force would detonate the mines. Not only would this blow up the road, but it would also destroy many neighboring villages. It therefore seemed impossible to capture the fortress. However, the general devised a simple plan. He divided his army into small groups and dispatched each group to the head of a different road. When all was ready he gave the signal and each group marched down a different road. Each group continued down its road to the fortress so that the entire army arrived together at the fortress at the same time. In this way, the general captured the fortress and overthrew the dictator (p. 351).

With this comparison in mind, 90 percent of the subjects were able to solve the problem. Why is it that people find the problem

FIGURE 2.1
Selected Research Results for Identifying Similarities and Differences

Synthesis Study	No. of Effect Sizes (ESs)	Ave. ES	Percentile Gain
Stone, 1983	22	.88	31
Stahl & Fairbanks, 1986[a]	9	1.39	42
	20	1.76	46
Ross, J. A., 1988	2	1.26	38
Lee, undated	2	1.28	39

[a] Two categories of effect sizes are listed for the Stahl and Fairbanks study because of the manner in which the effect sizes were reported. Readers should consult that study for more details.

so easy to solve after hearing the story? Quite simply, once the similarities are identified between the story, which is easy to understand, and the problem, which is difficult to solve, the solution becomes obvious. Figure 2.1 shows results from some of the major studies that have attempted to synthesize the research on identifying similarities and differences.

We can draw at least four salient generalizations from the research and theory in this area:

1. Presenting students with explicit guidance in identifying similarities and differences enhances students' understanding of and ability to use knowledge. Probably the most straightforward way to help students identify similarities and differences between topics is to simply present these similarities and differences to them. In fact,

a great deal of research attests to the effectiveness of this rather direct approach (see Chen, Yanowitz, & Daehler, 1996; Gholson, Smither, Buhrman, & Duncan, 1997; Newby, Ertmer, & Stepich, 1995; Reeves & Weisburg, 1994; Ross, B. H., 1984; Solomon, 1995). Being direct in pointing out similarities and differences, however, does not mean that instruction must be rigid or didactic. In many of the studies that support this generalization, the presentation of similarities and differences was accompanied by a great deal of rich discussion and inquiry on the part of students.

2. Asking students to independently identify similarities and differences enhances students' understanding of and ability to use knowledge. There is a strong research base supporting the effectiveness of having students identify similarities and differences without direct input from the teacher (see Chen, 1996; Flick, 1992; Gick & Holyoak, 1980; Mason, 1994, 1995; Mason & Sorzio, 1996). At first, this generalization might appear contradictory to the first, but it is not. Both "teacher-directed" and "student-directed" activities focused on identifying similarities and differences have their place in the classroom. One might assume that teacher-directed activities result in more homogeneous conclusions by students—the identification of "highly similar" similarities and differences by students; whereas, student-directed activities result in more heterogeneous conclusions by students. It would follow, then, that if a teacher wishes students to focus on specific similarities and differences, then she should provide students with a teacher-directed activity. If the teacher's goal is to stimulate divergence in students' thinking, however, then he should provide students with a student-directed activity.

3. Representing similarities and differences in graphic or symbolic form enhances students' understanding of and ability to use knowledge. One of the more powerful findings within this general category of instructional strategies is that graphic and symbolic representations of similarities and differences enhance students' understanding of content (see Chen, 1999; Cole & McLeod, 1999; Glynn & Takahashi, 1998; Lin, 1996; Mason, 1994). In Chapter 6, we discuss why the use of graphic and symbolic representations deepens knowledge. Here, we simply note that

their use greatly enhances students' ability to understand and generate similarities and differences.

4. Identification of similarities and differences can be accomplished in a variety of ways. The identification of similarities and differences is a highly robust activity. Research indicates that four different "forms" of this activity are highly effective:

- Comparing (see Chen, 1996; Chen et al., 1996; Flick, 1992; Ross, 1987; Solomon, 1995).
- Classifying (see Chi, Feltovich, & Glaser, 1981; English, 1997; Newby et al., 1995; Ripoll, 1999).
- Creating metaphors (see Chen, 1999; Cole & McLeod, 1999; Dagher, 1995; Gottfried, 1998; Mason, 1994, 1995).
- Creating analogies (see Alexander, 1984; Lee, n.d.; Ratterman & Gentner, 1998; Sternberg, 1977, 1978, 1979).

Figure 2.2 defines these forms.

Obviously, identifying similarities and differences is explicit in the process of comparing. It is also critical to classifying. To illustrate, when classifying, an individual first identifies similarities and differences within a set of elements and then organizes these elements into two or more categories, based on the identified similarities and differences. Creating a metaphor involves identifying abstract similarities and differences between two elements. Finally, creating analogies involves identifying how two pairs of elements are similar and different.

FIGURE 2.2

Definitions

Comparing is the process of identifying similarities and differences between or among things or ideas.

Classifying is the process of grouping things that are alike into categories on the basis of their characteristics.

Creating metaphors is the process of identifying a general or basic pattern in a specific topic and then finding another topic that appears to be quite different but that has the same general pattern.

Creating analogies is the process of identifying relationships between pairs of concepts— in other words, identifying relationships between relationships.

Note: Technically, the term *comparing* refers to the process of identifying similarities, and the term *contrasting* refers to the process of identifying differences. Most educators, however, use the term *comparing* to refer to both.

Classroom Practice in Identifying Similarities and Differences

Comparing

The key to an effective comparison is the identification of important characteristics. These characteristics are then used as the basis for which similarities and differences are identified.

Teacher-Directed Comparison Tasks. Although the process of comparing might seem simple, it is not. We suggest that teachers introduce the process of comparing by presenting students with highly structured tasks. This means that a teacher identifies for students the items they are to compare and the characteristics on which they are to base the comparison. These tasks, by definition, focus (even constrain) the type of conclusions students will reach. Consequently, they should be used when a teacher's goal is that all students obtain a general awareness of the same similarities and differences for the same characteristics. The following example shows a teacher-directed comparison task that a history teacher might present to students.

During "Women in History" month, Ms. Collier wanted her students to increase their understanding of the changing role of women in America. To begin the unit, she guided her students through a comparison of several First Ladies, including Martha Washington, Mary Todd Lincoln, Florence Kling Harding, Anna Eleanor Roosevelt, Mamie Eisenhower, and Hillary Rodham Clinton. Using information from the White House Web site (http://www.whitehouse. gov), students were to compare these women on the following characteristics: their backgrounds, their major responsibilities as First Lady, and things for which they were praised. Whereas students all focused on the same characteristics and the same first ladies, the information they gathered from the White House Web site was quite diverse. After they presented what they had found, all students agreed that they had gained a broad perspective on women's changing roles in American society.

Student-Directed Comparison Tasks.
Student-directed comparison tasks are
those in which the students select the characteristics on which the items are to be
compared, or the students select both the
items to compare and the characteristics on
which they are compared. Examples A and
B, respectively, depict these two versions of
student-directed comparison tasks.

A

> At the beginning of a unit on fairy tales, Mr.
> Webb asked each of his students to select
> two fairy tales with which they were familiar.
> He then introduced the major elements of
> literature that students would be applying to
> these fairy tales. As he introduced each ele-
> ment, such as universal theme, character-plot
> interactions, and point of view, Mr. Webb
> helped the students identify these character-
> istics in their two fairy tales. Students then
> were asked to compare their two fairy tales
> on the literary elements Mr. Webb had de-
> scribed. When reporting their results, stu-
> dents not only had to describe what they
> learned about the fairy tales they selected,
> but they also had to explain what they
> learned about the literary characteristics.

B

> Julia loved her year in Ms. Anchor's music
> class; she was even enjoying the final test. She
> had to select any four pieces of music and
> compare them according to any of the ele-
> ments of music that they had learned that
> year. Julia didn't own that many CDs, but stu-
> dents were allowed to come in after school
> and select from Ms. Anchor's incredible se-
> lection of music. She decided to compare a
> classical piece, a country-western song her
> mom liked, a current pop hit, and one of her
> favorite Disney songs. She even thought that

> listening to these tunes over and over as she
> did the comparison was going to be fun.

Graphic Organizers for Comparison.
Two types of graphic organizers are commonly used for comparison: the Venn diagram (Figure 2.3) and the comparison matrix (Figure 2.4).

As depicted in Figure 2.3, the Venn
diagram provides students with a visual display of the similarities and differences between two items. The similarities between
elements are listed in the intersection between the two circles. The differences are
listed in the parts of each circle that do not
intersect. Ideally, a new Venn diagram
should be completed for each characteristic
so that students can easily see how similar
and different the elements are for each
characteristic used in the comparison.

As Figure 2.4 illustrates, the comparison matrix provides for a more detailed
approach to comparison than does the
Venn diagram. Teachers use slightly more

FIGURE 2.3

Venn Diagram

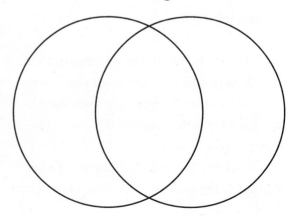

FIGURE 2.4

Comparison Matrix

Characteristics	Items to be compared				
	#1	#2	#3		
1.				Similarities	
				Differences	
2.				Similarities	
				Differences	
3.				Similarities	
				Differences	
4.				Similarities	
				Differences	

detailed directions for students when they use the comparison matrix. Example A contains directions to a task that involves the comparison matrix; Example B is a task that involves the Venn diagram.

A

Over the past several weeks, we have been learning about the explorers who helped settle the western United States. We have learned, for example, about the incredible expedition of Lewis and Clark and the exciting story of Zebulon Pike. You are now going to compare several explorers, using the comparison matrix. You may select some of your own characteristics for the comparison, but you must include the following: "who commissioned the exploration," "the kinds of risks involved," and "how people's lives have been influenced by the exploration."

After you have completed the center portion of the matrix, you are to create a new matrix using the same characteristics. This time, you will take this new matrix to your science class. Your teacher will present information to you about scientists who, in their own way, have engaged in exploration. For each characteristic in the comparison matrix, fill in information about these scientists. If you think of additional characteristics, add them to your matrix but also apply the new characteristics to the explorers matrix.

Finally, place the two matrixes side by side. Examine the information for all of the explorers, both from this class and from science class, and identify similarities and differences that strike you as important or interesting.

B

The first graders in Mrs. Bolton's class worked together to create a Venn Diagram to examine the similarities and differences between life today and life in the pioneer days (two of the diagrams are shown in Figure 2.5). Using these diagrams, one for each major characteristic, helped them to see clearly how their lives are similar to and different from the pioneers.

Classifying

Classifying involves organizing elements into groups based on their similarities. One of the critical elements of classifying is identifying the rules that govern class or category membership.

Teacher-Directed Classification Tasks. Teacher-directed classification tasks are those for which students are given the elements to classify and the categories into which the elements should be classified. In these tasks, the focus is on placing items into their appropriate categories and understanding why they belong in those categories. The following example depicts the use of a teacher-directed classification task in a physical education class.

> Mr. Trelfa wanted his elementary physical education students to increase their general understanding of sports. He provided them with an ongoing task to be completed as they watched the Olympic events, both at home and at school. The students were given a complete list of events in the Olympics and were asked to classify them into the following categories:
>
> ◆ Events that require mainly strength and agility.
> ◆ Events that require mainly precision and accuracy.

> ◆ Events that have about equal requirements for strength/agility and precision/accuracy.
>
> In class, students were asked to describe how they categorized events and defend why specific events belonged in specific categories.

Student-Directed Classification Tasks. Student-directed classification tasks are those in which students are given the items to classify but must form the categories themselves. Additionally, students can be asked to generate both the items to classify and the categories into which they are organized. The following example shows a student-directed classification task in which students have control over the items they categorize and the categories into which they place items.

> An advanced placement literature class had just finished the last book they were to read for the year. As a culminating activity, Mrs. Blake, a teacher many students had for two years, asked them to do the following activity, both to use what they know and to discover some new connections they had possibly missed through the years.

> With a partner, make a list of as many characters as you can recall from the books we have read. Then, classify them into categories of your choosing. Stay away from obvious categories, such as gender or nationality. Use categories that show your understanding of character development. When you are finished, reclassify the characters, using new categories. Find another pair of students and discuss your work.

FIGURE 2.5

Venn Diagram: Pioneer Days and Today

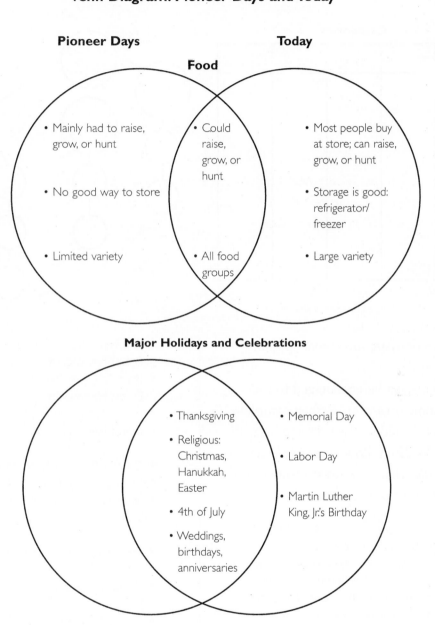

Pioneer Days **Today**

Food

- Mainly had to raise, grow, or hunt
- No good way to store
- Limited variety

- Could raise, grow, or hunt
- All food groups

- Most people buy at store; can raise, grow, or hunt
- Storage is good: refrigerator/ freezer
- Large variety

Major Holidays and Celebrations

- Thanksgiving
- Religious: Christmas, Hanukkah, Easter
- 4th of July
- Weddings, birthdays, anniversaries

- Memorial Day
- Labor Day
- Martin Luther King, Jr's Birthday

Graphic Organizers for Classification. Figure 2.6 shows two popular graphic organizers for classification. The graphic organizer on the left (which looks like a boxed table) is most appropriate when all categories are equal in terms of their level of generality. The graphic organizer on the right (a "bubble" chart) is better used when

FIGURE 2.6

Graphic Organizers for Classification

Categories

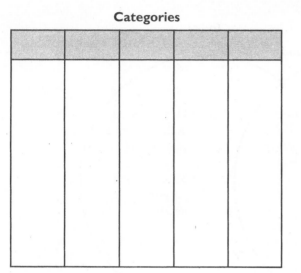

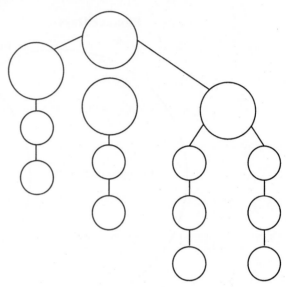

some categories are more general than others.

Students can be encouraged to use these graphic organizers as they complete their teacher- and student-directed classification tasks. The following example describes a task that requires students to use a classification graphic organizer.

> The following characters are from books we have read in class this year. Using the graphic organizer for classification, organize these characters into two or more categories. Be prepared to explain the rules that govern membership in each category and why particular characters belong in that category.
>
> ♦ Ponyboy Curtis in *The Outsiders* by S. E. Hinton
> ♦ Johnnycake in *The Outsiders* by S. E. Hinton
> ♦ Cherry Valance in *The Outsiders* by S. E. Hinton

♦ Jake Barnes in *The Sun Also Rises* by Ernest Hemingway
♦ Brett Ashley in *The Sun Also Rises* by Ernest Hemingway
♦ Pedro Romero in *The Sun Also Rises* by Ernest Hemingway

♦ Celie in *The Color Purple* by Alice Walker
♦ Mr. in *The Color Purple* by Alice Walker
♦ Shug Avery in *The Color Purple* by Alice Walker

♦ Ethan Frome in *Ethan Frome* by Edith Wharton
♦ Zenobia Frome in *Ethan Frome* by Edith Wharton
♦ Mattie Silver in *Ethan Frome* by Edith Wharton

♦ Gene Forrester in *A Separate Peace* by John Knowles
♦ Finny in *A Separate Peace* by John Knowles

- Antonio Marez in *Bless Me, Ultima* by Rudolfo Anaya
- Ultima in *Bless Me, Ultima* by Rudolfo Anaya

- Scout in *To Kill a Mockingbird* by Harper Lee
- Atticus Finch in *To Kill a Mockingbird* by Harper Lee
- Boo Radley in *To Kill a Mockingbird* by Harper Lee

Metaphors

The key to constructing metaphors is to realize that the two items in the metaphor are connected by an abstract or nonliteral relationship. For example, "Love is a rose" is a metaphor. On the surface, love and a rose have no obvious relationship. At an abstract level, however, they do. Here's how one can say love is a rose!

Literal: **Rose:** The blossom is sweet to smell and pleasant to touch, but if you touch the thorns, they can stick you.

Abstract: Something is wonderful and you want to go near it, but if you get too close, you might get hurt.

Literal: **Love:** Makes you feel happy, but the person you love can end up hurting you.

It is at the abstract level only that *love* and *rose* appear related. It follows, then, that instructional strategies involving metaphors

should always address the abstract relationship between the elements.

Teacher-Directed Metaphors. Teacher-directed metaphors are those in which the teacher provides the first element of the metaphor and the abstract relationship. This structure provides a "scaffold" on which students can build. The following example depicts a teacher-directed metaphor activity in the context of a science class.

Mrs. Blair started her science unit on extinction by handing out an article about the Dodo bird (see next page).

Mrs. Blair then guided the students through a process of identifying the general, abstract pattern from the information about the Dodo bird. As a group, they extracted the following pattern:

1. Something was thriving in a specific environment.
2. This thing changed over time because of changes in its surroundings. Some of the changes actually limited it in some ways.
3. Yet another influence came along and cut off what it needed to survive and destroyed where it used to exist. Because of its limitations, there was no way it could move to a new place.
4. The thing no longer exists.

Mrs. Blair then asked students to use this general pattern, which was derived from the story of the Dodo bird, to identify something else that fit the pattern.

Student-Directed Metaphor Tasks. Once students become familiar with the concept of an abstract pattern or relationship, they might be provided with tasks in

The Dodo Bird—A Lesson in Extinction

The Dodo bird was first sighted around 1600 on Mauritius, an island in the Indian Ocean. It was extinct less than eighty years later. The Dodo's stubby wings and heavy, ungainly body tell us that the bird could not fly. Moreover, its breastbone was too small to support the huge pectoral muscles a bird this size would need to fly. Yet scientists believe that the Dodo evolved from a bird capable of flight. When an ancestor of the Dodo landed on Mauritius, it found a habitat with plenty of food and no predators. Because there was no reason for Dodos to leave the ground, they eventually lost their ability to fly. Other factors also contributed to the Dodo birds' extinction.

For example, many birds were eaten by the Dutch sailors who discovered them. However, the two most influential factors in terms of the Dodo birds' extinction were the destruction of the forest (which cut off the Dodo's food supply), and the animals that the sailors brought with them, including cats, rats, and pigs. These animals destroyed Dodo nests.

Scientists at the American Museum of Natural History and other institutions around the world have learned from the Dodo bird. They hope that the lesson of the Dodo can help prevent the extinction of other forms of animal life and aid us in preserving the diversity of life on earth.

FIGURE 2.7

Graphic Organizer for Metaphors

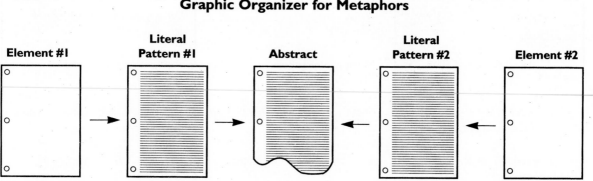

Element #1	Literal Pattern #1	Abstract	Literal Pattern #2	Element #2

which they are presented with one element of a metaphor and asked to identify the second element and describe the abstract relationship. Such tasks are more student-directed. The following example shows such a task in the context of a science class.

> Two science students were standing in front of the class pointing to the diagram of the Starship *Enterprise* (from *Star Trek*) as they presented their project. Their assignment was to identify the major structures of a cell and describe the function of each. They were then to restate the information in more general, abstract terms and, finally, to identify another system that is similar to the cell, at an abstract level. These two students had selected the *Enterprise* as the second element of the metaphor, and identified the following abstract pattern connecting a cell with the starship:

Cell	General, Abstract	Enterprise
Nucleus	The part that runs the system	The bridge
Selectively permeable membrane	Part that keeps out bad things and lets in the good	Transporter Room

In a detailed and articulate way, students described how each aspect of the cell was like a feature of the *Enterprise*.

A Graphic Organizer for Metaphors. Graphic organizers are not as common with metaphors as they are with comparison and classification tasks. Figure 2.7 shows a graphic organizer that can be used to provide a visual representation of the nature and function of a metaphor.

The key aspect of this graphic organizer is that it depicts the fact that two elements might have somewhat different literal patterns, but share a common abstract pattern. Using the graphic organizer, students can fill in the elements of a metaphor, the literal pattern for each element and the abstract pattern that connects them. The following is an example of how a teacher might adapt this graphic organizer.

> Mrs. Zeno was trying to get her primary students to understand the steps of writing a paragraph. She started by writing the phrase "Making a Sandwich" (see next page) in the

Making a Sandwich	Another Way to Say It	Writing a Paragraph
What are you hungry for?	What is my goal?	What is the topic or purpose of the paragraph?
What kind of bread?	What will hold it together?	What will be my first and last sentences?
What will I put in the sandwich that will make it tasty?	What will go in the middle that will all go together?	What sentences do I need to help the topic of my paragraph?
Shall I add something to make it better? Pickles? Mustard? Banana slices?	How can I make it even better?	What can I do to make it more interesting or easier to understand? Adjectives? Another detail?

box on the left, and the phrase "Writing a Paragraph" in the box on the far right. She then wrote the questions you might ask to make a satisfying sandwich. As a class, they translated these questions to a more abstract form in the box labeled "Another Way to Say It." With these in place, the class identified the questions they would need to answer to write a good paragraph.

Analogies

Like metaphors, analogies help us see how seemingly dissimilar things are similar, increasing our understanding of new information. Typically, analogies take the form A:B::C:D (read as, "A is to B as C is to D"). For example:

◆ hot:cold::night:day ("hot is to cold as night is to day"); *cold* and *day* are opposites as are *hot* and *night*.

◆ carpenter:hammer::painter:brush ("carpenter is to hammer as painter is to brush"); *hammer* and *brush* are tools used by a *carpenter* and a *painter*, respectively.

Analogies are probably the most complex format for identifying similarities and differences in that they deal with "relationships between relationships." Just like other forms of identifying similarities and differences, analogies can be used in teacher-directed or student-directed activities.

Teacher-Directed Analogies. By definition, teacher-directed analogies are those for which students are provided a great deal of structure. For example, a teacher might present the following analogy:

thermometer is to temperature
as
odometer is to distance

The teacher would then ask students to explain how the relationship between thermometer and temperature is similar to the relationship between odometer and distance. Specifically, a thermometer measures incremental changes in temperature and an odometer measures incremental changes in distance. In addition, a teacher might present students with one element missing within the four parts of an analogy. Examples A and B depict these two forms of teacher-directed analogy tasks, respectively.

A

The following analogies were included on a study sheet students were given to help them study for their final exam.

Oxygen is to humans
as
carbon dioxide is to plants

tsunami is to wave
as
earthquake is to tremor

core is to earth
as
nucleus is to atom

frequency is to sound
as
ampere is to electricity

Newton is to force and motion
as
Bernouli is to air pressure

B

A math teacher presented students with the following analogy problems to help increase their understanding of math concepts.

eighty is to eight
as
dime is to _____

pint is to quart
as
1000 lb. is to _____

acute is to triangle
as
square is to _____

circumference is to circle
as
perimeter is to _____

½ is to fraction
as
5 is to _____

mean is to average
as
mode is to _____

Student-Directed Analogies. Student-directed analogy tasks ask students to provide more elements of an analogy than do teacher-directed analogy tasks. For example, a teacher might present students with the elements of the first pair of an analogy and ask them to generate the elements of the second pair. Obviously, this type of analogy task would require much more explanation from the student. The following example shows student-directed analogy tasks that might be presented in a literature unit.

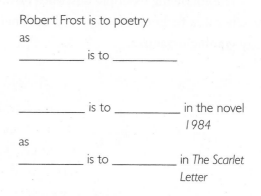

Robert Frost is to poetry
as
_____ is to _____

_____ is to _____ in the novel
1984
as
_____ is to _____ in The Scarlet
Letter

FIGURE 2.8

Graphic Organizer for Analogies

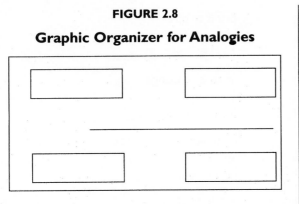

FIGURE 2.9

Graphic Organizer for Analogies in Use

| thermometer | is to | temperature |

Relationship: measures incremental changes in something

as | odometer | is to | distance |

Figure 2.8 shows a graphic organizer that might be used with students to help them understand the nature of analogies. Again, students would use the graphic organizer to fill the elements of an analogy, as Figure 2.9 shows.

The following example describes how a teacher in a technology class used the analogy graphic organizer.

With his class, Mr. Waters has been discussing the impact the computer has had on modern society. As a way of deepening their thinking about this topic, he presents students with the following analogy graphic organizer:

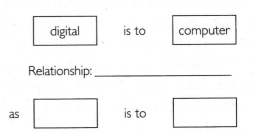

Relationship: _____

Even though the elements in the first pair of the graphic organizers have been filled out, Mr. Waters spends some time discussing the relationship between these elements with the class. After the discussion, students work in groups of three to fill out the elements in the second pair of the analogy graphic organizer. The next day, each group presents their completed analogy graphic organizer and explains and defends the relationship linking the two pairs.

◆ ◆ ◆

Identifying similarities and differences can play out in many ways in the classroom. Students can be engaged in tasks that involve comparisons, classifications, metaphors, and analogies. In addition, these tasks can be either more teacher directed or student directed.

3

Summarizing and Note Taking

In previous years, Mrs. Zimmers taught her middle school unit on mythology by assigning the students a selection of myths to read and asking them to construct their own myths using a story structure in which many of the characters undergo dramatic changes. While the students often enjoyed the storytelling nature of the task, they seemed to miss the deep historical importance of the myths to the people who created them. This year she had a plan to change things. To gain a deeper understanding about the history of ancient Greece, students were asked to read two essays and view a short film on Greek mythology. Additionally, students were asked to summarize each essay as homework. Finally, Mrs. Zimmers asked students to turn in the notes they took during the film.

Mrs. Zimmers was taken aback with what she received. When she read the first summaries, she realized that many students did not really summarize the information or did not understand the nature and purpose of a summary. They simply reworded information from the text and made no attempt to translate it into a synthesized form. To her dismay, she concluded that her students did not know how to summarize. Mrs. Zimmers set for herself the goal of teaching her students a specific summarizing strategy. Mrs. Zimmers also realized that she would have to teach note-taking strategies and skills. Most of the students took far too few notes, although a couple of students tried to record everything they heard or read.

After realizing a skill weakness in her students, Mrs. Zimmers has chosen to explicitly teach two of the most useful academic skills students can have: summarizing and note taking. We have assigned these skills to the same instructional category because they both require students to distill information into a parsimonious, synthesized form.

Research and Theory on Summarizing

Summarizing has a robust and long history of research. Figure 3.1 reports findings from some of the studies that have attempted to synthesize the research on summarizing.

Researchers Valerie Anderson and Suzanne Hidi have provided highly useful reviews of the rather voluminous literature base in summarizing (see Anderson, V., & Hidi, 1988/1989; Hidi & Anderson, 1987). We can extract at least three generalizations from this research:

1. To effectively summarize, students must delete some information, substitute some information, and keep some information. This generalization springs from the work of cognitive psychologists like Walter Kintsch and Teun van Dijk (see Kintsch, 1979; van Dijk, 1980) who have studied the basic cognitive mechanisms involved in summarizing. To illustrate, consider Figure 3.2, which contains a sample passage about the photographic process.

If you were to read this passage with the purpose of summarizing it, your mind would quite naturally engage in three activities: (1) deleting things, (2) substituting things, and (3) keeping things. To obtain a sense of the outcome of these three processes, consider part B of Figure 3.2, which shows how a reader might summarize this passage.

FIGURE 3.1
Research Results for Summarizing Strategies

Synthesis Study	No. of Effect Sizes (ESs)	Ave. ES	Percentile Gain
Pflaum, Walberg, Karegianes, & Rasher, 1980[a]	2	.62	23
	2	.73	27
Crismore, 1985	100	1.04	35
Rosenshine & Meister, 1994	10	.88	31
Hattie, Biggs, & Purdie, 1996	15	.88	31
Rosenshine, Meister, & Chapman, 1996	16	.87	31
Raphael & Kirschner, 1985	3	1.80	47

[a] Two categories of effect sizes are listed for the Pflaum et al. study because of the manner in which the effect sizes were reported. Readers should consult that study for more details.

FIGURE 3.2

Exercise in Summarizing

A	B
The Photographic Process	**Macro-structure of the Photographic Process**

A

The word *photography* comes from the Greek word meaning "drawing with light.". . . Light is the most essential ingredient in photography. Nearly all forms of photography are based on the fact that certain chemicals are *photosensitive*—that is, they change in some way when exposed to light. Photosensitive materials abound in nature; plants that close their blooms at night are one example. The films used in photography depend on a limited number of chemical compounds that darken when exposed to light. The compounds most widely used today are silver and chemicals called *halogens* (usually bromine, chlorine, or iodine).

B

~~The word *photography* comes from Greek words and means "drawing with light.". . .~~ Light is the most essential ingredient in photography. ~~Nearly all forms of photography are based on the fact that certain chemicals are *photosensitive*—that is, they change in some way when exposed to light. Photosensitive materials abound in nature; plants that close their blooms at night are one example.~~ Photography depends on chemical crystals that ~~The films used in photography depend on a limited number of chemical compounds that~~ darken when exposed to light. ~~The compounds most widely used today are silver and chemicals called *halogens* (usually bromine, chlorine, or iodine).~~

Source: From "Photography." In *Microsoft Encarta Encyclopedia 99*, CD-ROM, Microsoft, 1999.

Note how much of the content has been deleted in Figure 3.2B. The reader simply decided that this information is not central to the overall meaning of the passage. Also note that one term has been substituted for a term in the original text—the term *crystals* has been substituted for the term *compounds*. In a summary, the "substitute" terms can be more general or more specific than those in the text. Finally, note that a few phrases and sentences that seem to convey the key information have been kept. This final, parsimonious synthesis of the information is technically referred to as the "macro-structure" for the information.

2. **To effectively delete, substitute, and keep information, students must analyze the information at a fairly deep level.** Although the mental operations involved in summarizing—deleting, substituting, keeping—seem quite simple, they demand a fair amount of analysis of the information being summarized. To illustrate using Figure 3.2 again, it requires no small amount of analytic thinking to conclude that the information about the origin of the word *photography* is not critically important, but the information that light is an essential ingredient is. In fact, in their synthesis of research, Borak Rosenshine and his colleagues

(see Rosenshine & Meister, 1994; Rosenshine, Meister, & Chapman, 1996) concluded that strategies that emphasize the analytic aspect of summarizing, produce the most powerful effects in terms of students' ability to summarize.

3. Being aware of the explicit structure of information is an aid to summarizing information. Most writers present information in the context of an explicit structure, and the more a person is aware of this explicit structure, the better she is able to summarize the information. This generalization was brought to the attention of educators by the work of psychologists like Bonnie Meyer (see Meyer, 1975; Meyer & Freedle, 1984). To illustrate, assume you are about to read an article in an education journal on the topic of effective discipline strategies. Even before reading the article, you would know that it will probably take a certain form. You would expect there to be an introductory section explaining why effective disciplinary strategies are important; there would probably be a section discussing what has been done in the past. Then, there would be a section describing the strategies the author considers most useful. At the end, there probably would be some type of summary statement. An awareness of this structure helps you identify which parts of the article to attend to the most. This knowledge helps you summarize the information. In general, research has demonstrated that making students aware of the specific structure in information helps them summarize that information (see Armbruster, Anderson, & Ostertag, 1987; Raphael & Kirschner, 1985).

Classroom Practice in Summarizing

The "Rule-Based" Strategy

One summarizing strategy developed by Brown, Campione, and Day (1981) is referred to as a rule-based summary strategy. As the name implies, the strategy is one of following a set of rules or steps that produce a summary. Those rules are as follows:

- Delete trivial material that is unnecessary to understanding.
- Delete redundant material.
- Substitute superordinate terms for lists (e.g., "flowers" for "daisies, tulips, and roses").
- Select a topic sentence, or invent one if it is missing.

It is fairly easy to see that these rules closely mirror the cognitive process of summarizing as described in Generalization 1—deleting, substituting, keeping. In effect, the rules given students are the very things they have to do to produce a summary. Simply directing students what to do, however, is not the same as showing them how to do it. To make these rules "come alive" for students, a teacher might initially

---

FIGURE 3.3

Summarizing Strategy: Sample Passage

Why Does Studying Solar Wind Tell Us About the Origin of Our Solar System?

Most scientists believe our solar system was formed 4.6 billion years ago with the gravitational collapse of the solar nebula, a cloud of interstellar gas, dust, and ice created from previous generations of stars. As time went on the grains of ice and dust bumped into and stuck to one another, eventually forming the planets, moons, comets, and asteroids as we know them today.

How this transition from the solar nebula to planets took place has both fascinated and mystified scientists. Why did some planets, like Venus, develop thick, poisonous atmospheres, while others, like Earth, became hospitable to life? Partial answers are available from the study of the chemical composition of the solar system bodies, which scientists find are significantly different from one another. This information helps them model various processes for planet formation, but they are still hampered by one major question: What was the original solar nebula made of?

Our sun may contain the answer. It contains over 99 percent of all the material in the solar system and, while its interior has been modified by nuclear reactions, its outer layers are believed to be composed of the same material as the original solar nebula. By collecting and studying solar wind, the material flung from the sun, scientists may find more answers to this mysterious puzzle.

---

demonstrate them in some detail. The following example shows how a teacher might do this.

Mr. Newton is trying to walk students through the rule-based summarizing strategy in the context of a science unit. He begins by presenting them with a passage on the origin of the solar system (see Figure 3.3).

He first asks students to read the passage silently. After they read the passage, Mr. Newton explains that he is going to use it to demonstrate the "rule-based strategy" for summarizing which he introduced them to the previous day. He talks them through the process as follows:

"I'm going to think aloud as I apply the rules of this strategy. See if my thinking makes sense to you.

"The rules say to 'delete trivial material, to delete redundant material, and to substitute superordinate terms for lists.' The first paragraph is almost all background, but it doesn't seem trivial. There are, however, a couple of lists. Let's see, for '*interstellar gas, dust, and ice*' I'll substitute '*interstellar material.*' For '*planets, moons, comets, and asteroids*' I'll substitute '*heavenly bodies.*' Also, I see something redundant: The '*solar nebula*' and the '*cloud of interstellar material created from previous generations of stars*' are the same thing, so I'll delete one of them. And come to think of it, the expression '*bumped into*' is a little trivial and a little redundant. I think I can take it out, too. Here's my first paragraph now:"

Most scientists believe our solar system was formed 4.6 billion years ago with the gravitational collapse of the solar nebula. As time went on grains from the solar nebula stuck to one another, eventually forming the heavenly bodies we know today.

"Now I'll apply the rules to the second paragraph. Hmm, I don't see any lists for which I could substitute a superordinate term, but *'fascinated and mystified'* is a little redundant. I'll just say *'intrigued'* which sort of combines them. Also, the examples about Venus and the Earth, while interesting, aren't necessary to my understanding of the paragraph. I think I'll take them out.

"The rest of the paragraph explains what scientists already know and what they need to know. It's not really trivial, but for a summary I'm going to try and say it more simply. I'll take the part that says *'partial answers are available from the study of the chemical composition of the solar system bodies, which scientists find are significantly different from one another. This information helps them model various processes for planet formation, but they are still hampered by one major question: What was the original solar nebula made of?'* and just say *'Scientists have some of the answers but they really need to know what the original solar system was made of'.* How's this?"

How this transition from the solar nebula to planets took place has intrigued scientists. They have some of the answers but they really need to know what the original solar nebula was made of.

"The third paragraph is full of interesting information. How can I apply the rules here? Is anything redundant, trivial, or unnecessary to my understanding?

"The first sentence says *'our sun may contain the answer.'* Wow, that's important so I'll keep it. The second sentence explains why the sun may contain the answer. Only part of that sentence—*'its outer layers are believed to be composed of the same material as the original solar nebula'*—is necessary to my understanding so I can take out the rest. In the last sentence, *'solar wind'* and *'the material flung from the sun'* are the same thing so I'll keep only one. Now I've got:"

Our sun may contain the answer. Its outer layers are believed to be composed of the same material as the original solar nebula. By collecting and studying the material flung from the sun, scientists may find more answers to this mysterious puzzle.

"Finally, I can put it all together. Do the three new paragraphs make sense? Hmm, I think my use of the term *'solar nebula'* is a little redundant. I'll take it out where I can without losing clarity. What do you think of my final summary?"

Most scientists believe our solar system was formed 4.6 billion years ago with the gravitational collapse of the solar nebula. As time went on grains from the solar nebula stuck to one another, eventually forming the heavenly bodies we know today.

How this transition took place has intrigued scientists. They have some of the answers but they really need to know what the original solar nebula was made of.

Our sun may contain the answer. Its outer layers are believed to be composed of the same material as the original solar nebula. By collecting and studying the material flung from the sun, scientists may find more answers to this mysterious puzzle.

After this detailed description of his own thinking, Mr. Newton has students try out the rule-based summarizing strategy on their own using a different passage from the textbook.

Summary Frames

Summary frames are direct applications of Generalization 3. A summary frame is a series of questions that the teacher provides to students. These questions are designed to highlight the critical elements for specific types of information. We present six types of summary frames in this chapter:

1. The Narrative Frame
2. The Topic-Restriction-Illustration Frame
3. The Definition Frame
4. The Argumentation Frame
5. The Problem/Solution Frame
6. The Conversation Frame

Each frame captures the basic structure of a different type of text. To illustrate, consider Figures 3.4–3.9. Also note the questions that go with each frame.

FIGURE 3.4

The Narrative Frame

The narrative or story frame is commonly found in fiction and contains the following elements:

1. **Characters**: the characteristics of the main characters in the story.
2. **Setting**: the time, place, and context in which the information took place.
3. **Initiating event**: the event that starts the action rolling in the story.
4. **Internal response**: how the main characters react emotionally to the initiating event.
5. **Goal**: what the main characters decide to do as a reaction to the initiating event (the goal they set).
6. **Consequence**: how the main characters try to accomplish the goal.
7. **Resolution**: how the goal turns out.

Components 3–7 are sometimes repeated to create what is called an *episode*.

> **Frame Questions**
>
> 1. Who are the main characters and what distinguishes them from others?
> 2. When and where did the story take place? What were the circumstances?
> 3. What prompted the action in the story?
> 4. How did the characters express their feelings?
> 5. What did the main characters decide to do? Did they set a goal, and, if so, what was it?
> 6. How did the main characters try to accomplish their goal(s)?
> 7. What were the consequences?

The following example shows how a 1st grade teacher used the Narrative Frame (Figure 3.4) to teach her students about summarization.

Mrs. Mason used the narrative frame to help her 1st graders summarize the story, "Inktomi Lost His Eyes" (a story from the Assiniboine tribe). First she introduced the frame questions, and told the students to think about them as she read the story aloud. Then she read the story again. This time, however, she occasionally stopped to let the students answer the frame questions as a class. Here are the questions and the answers generated by the students:

1. Who are the main characters and what distinguishes them from others? Inktomi, the curious little boy and the singing bird that could "throw" his eyes.

2. When and where did the story take place? What were the circumstances? The Assiniboine legend takes place in the forest where the little boy was walking.

3. What prompted the action in the story? The boy heard the bird sing in his language and then "throw" his eyes and sing them back.

4. How did the characters express their feelings? The little boy wanted the trick so he would be admired and have power. He asked the bird for the trick.

5. What did the main characters decide to do? Did they set a goal, and, if so, what was it? The boy abused the trick by not following the bird's warning. He lost his sight and set out to get it back.

6. How did the main characters try to accomplish their goal(s)? The little boy asked other animals to help him find the bird.

7. What were the consequences? The little boy got his sight back, but also learned to not be vain.

Finally, Mrs. Mason and the students used their answers to the frame questions to write the following summary:

In this Assiniboine legend that takes place in a forest, a curious boy heard a bird sing, and then "throw" his eyes, and sing them back again. The little boy, who wanted to be admired and have power, asked the bird for the trick. The boy did not follow the bird's warning, lost his sight, and set out to get it back. The little boy asked forest animals to help get his sight back. In this lesson, the boy learned to not be vain.

Proceed to the next frame

FIGURE 3.5

The Topic-Restriction-Illustration Frame

T-R-I stands for topic, restriction, and illustration. This pattern is commonly found in expository material. The T-R-I frame contains the following elements:

Topic (T)—general statement about the topic to be discussed
Restriction (R)—limits the information in some way
Illustrations (I)—exemplifies the topic or restriction

The T-R-I pattern can have a number of restrictions and additional illustrations.

Frame Questions

1. T—What is the general statement or topic?
2. R—What information narrows or restricts the general statement or topic?
3. I—What examples illustrate the topic or restriction?

Figure 3.5 shows another summarization technique, the Topic-Restriction-Illustration Frame. The following example shows how a teacher used the frame to teach students in a geography class:

Mr. Burke uses the T-R-I frame in his 7th grade geography class as he presents information about the topic of interdependence of trade among nations. He first presents students with the following frame questions:

1. T—What is the meaning of "trade"?
2. R—How does the definition of trade vary from different countries (e.g., in industrialized or in developing countries)?
3. I—What examples illustrate this?
4. R—How can a short-term positive balance of trade negatively affect long-term trade in developing countries?
5. I—What examples illustrate this?

Next, in lecture format, he presents information about trade. Occasionally, he stops and asks students to fill in answers to the frame questions based on the information he has presented. For homework, students translate the answers to their frame questions into a summary paragraph.

FIGURE 3.6

The Definition Frame

The purpose of a definition frame is to describe a particular concept and identify subordinate concepts. Definition patterns contain the following elements:

1. Term—the subject to be defined.
2. Set—the general category to which the term belongs.
3. Gross characteristics—those characteristics that separate the term from other elements in the set.
4. Minute differences—those different classes of objects that fall directly beneath the term.

> **Frame Questions**
>
> 1. What is being defined?
> 2. To which general category does the item belong?
> 3. What characteristics separate the item from other things in the general category?
> 4. What are some different types or classes of the item being defined?

A third type of summary technique, the Definition Frame (Figure 3.6), is illustrated by students in a life sciences class in the following example.

Students in Mrs. Miller's 3rd grade life science class are studying about monotremes. This particular day she is showing a film. To guide their viewing of the film, Mrs. Miller presents students with the following frame questions with some answers filled in:

1. What is being defined? *A monotreme.*
2. To which general category do monotremes belong? *Mammals.*

3. What characteristics separate monotremes from other things in the general category?

4. What are some different types of monotremes?

Mrs. Miller explains to her students that all of the answers to the frame questions can be found in the film, but they will have to identify which information answers a specific question and which information does not. Students watch the film with an eye toward answering the questions. When the film is over, Mrs. Miller organizes students into groups where they compare their answers and construct a summary statement about monotremes as a group.

FIGURE 3.7

The Argumentation Frame

Argumentation frames contain information designed to support a claim. They contain the following elements:

1. **Evidence**: information that leads to a claim.
2. **Claim**: the assertion that something is true—the claim that is the focal point of the argument.
3. **Support**: examples of or explanations for the claim.
4. **Qualifier**: a restriction on the claim or evidence for the claim.

Frame Questions

1. What information is presented that leads to a claim?
2. What is the basic statement or claim that is the focus of the information?
3. What examples or explanations are presented to support this claim?
4. What concessions are made about the claim?

In a fourth type of summarizing technique, the Argumentation Frame (Figure 3.7), students in a literature class answer questions that clarify an article the teacher asks them to read.

Mrs. Van Den Wildenberg uses the argumentation frame as a way to help students summarize an article they are assigned to read about Mark Twain in her sophomore literature class. She first presents the argumentation questions and then asks students to answer them in writing as she reads the article. One student, Maurie, answers the argumentation frame questions in the following way:

1. What information is presented that leads to a claim? The author says that a true American author should exhibit the key characteristics of the American culture. These include: pioneering, rebelliousness, humor, and casualness.

2. What is the basic claim or focus of the information? Greg chose Mark Twain as the "quintessential American" author.

3. What examples or explanations are presented to support this claim? Mark Twain's various works along with literary criticisms of his works are presented.

4. What concessions are made about the claim? Other authors' works are also mentioned as exemplifying key American characteristics.

When all students have answered the frame questions, Mrs. Van Den Wildenberg organizes students into groups where they compare their answers and construct a group summary.

FIGURE 3.8

The Problem/Solution Frame

Problem/solution frames introduce a problem and then identify one or more solutions to the problem.

Problem: A statement of something that has happened or might happen that is problematic.
Solution: A description of one possible solution.
Solution: A statement of another possible solution.
Solution: A statement of another possible solution.
Solution: Identification of the solution with the greatest chance of success.

> **Frame Questions**
>
> 1. What is the problem?
> 2. What is a possible solution?
> 3. What is another possible solution?
> 4. Which solution has the best chance of succeeding?

The fifth type of summary framework is the Problem/Solution Frame (Figure 3.8); its use is shown in the following 6th grade example.

Mr. Farrington is teaching a unit to his 6th graders called, "Monterrey—The Big Cleanup." After a short introductory lecture about the biggest manufacturing center of Mexico, he shows some slides and videotape depicting the problems that have been caused by mining. Because tailings from the mining process have caused land and water pollution, the government seeks solutions to their waste material problems. Mr. Farrington sets up various demonstration information centers for the students. Each center exemplifies a way to separate waste materials from earth or water. After visiting all of the centers, students answer the problem/solution frame questions. To summarize, the students use a graphic representation to show the best ways to extract waste material.

FIGURE 3.9

The Conversation Frame

A conversation is a verbal interchange between two or more people. Commonly, a conversation has the following components:

1. **Greeting**: some acknowledgment that the parties have not seen each other for a while.
2. **Inquiry:** a question about some general or specific topic.
3. **Discussion**: an elaboration or analysis of the topic. Commonly included in the discussion are one or more of the following:

   Assertions: statements of facts by the speaker.
   Requests: statements that solicit actions from the listener.
   Promises: statements that assert that the speaker will perform certain actions.
   Demands: statements that identify specific actions to be taken by the listener.
   Threats: statements that specify consequences to the listener if commands are not followed.
   Congratulations: statements that indicate the value the speaker puts on something done by the listener.

4. **Conclusion**: the conversation ends in some way.

Frame Questions

1. How did the members of the conversation greet each other?
2. What question or topic was insinuated, revealed, or referred to?
3. How did their discussion progress?
   Did either person state facts?
   Did either person make a request of the other?
   Did either person demand a specific action of the other?
   Did either person threaten specific consequences if a demand was
   not met?
   Did either person indicate that he/she valued something that the other
   had done?
4. How did the conversation conclude?

Sometimes information comes in the form of a conversation, or dialogue, in a story. The following language arts example shows students using the Conversation Frame (Figure 3.9) as a summarization tool.

Mrs. Washington believes that teaching students how to summarize conversations will help them understand both character and plot as revealed in conversations. To prepare her 2nd grade students, she teaches them the conversation frame and helps them to practice with simple text from "The Billy

Goats Gruff." Mrs. Washington leads the discussion and calls on students to respond. She records the answers as follows:

1. How did the members of the conversation greet each other?
   The mean troll grunted at Little Billy Goat Gruff. The little goat just gave his name.
2. What questions or topic was insinuated, revealed or referred to?
   The topic of the conversation was about whether the goat could cross the bridge.
3. How did their discussion progress?
   The troll threatened to eat the goat if the goat crossed his bridge.
4. What was the conclusion?
   The goat talked the troll into waiting for his bigger brother.

Using the group answers to the conversation frame questions, the whole class then summarizes the story.

Gradually, Mrs. Washington increases the complexity of the conversations the students summarize until they are ready to try an example from Sherlock Holmes. She warns the students that the conversations in the text are long, but that summarizing them is the key to understanding the story. The class works together on the first Holmes example, a conversation in "A Study in Scarlet," during which Dr. Watson and Sherlock Holmes meet each other for the first time. To their surprise, students are able to summarize the conversation quite well using the frame questions.

Reciprocal Teaching

Reciprocal teaching, developed by Palincsar and Brown (1984, 1985), is one of the best researched strategies available to teachers (see Rosenshine & Meister, 1994).

The strategy involves four components: summarizing, questioning, clarifying, and predicting. Figure 3.10 briefly describes these phases.

Although reciprocal teaching begins with the generation of a summary statement, it might be considered a "first draft" of a summary. The questioning, clarifying, and predicting phases of reciprocal teaching helps students engage in the analysis activities described in Generalization 2 above. Reciprocal teaching, then, can be considered a strategy that provides for a deep level of understanding necessary for an effective summary. The following example shows how a teacher might use reciprocal teaching in a music class.

Collin was selected to be the leader in his reciprocal teaching group. After the students in Collin's group read the first few paragraphs in the passage the teacher had taken from the Internet, "Sound Is Energy" (http:// tqjunior. advanced.org/5116/), Collin explained the terms *tone* and *harmonics*. He also did a nice job summarizing the information about sound waves. The questions he asked the class about *frequency* and *hertz* indicated that most students understood that part of the passage. The "clarifying" part of reciprocal teaching was easy for him because he couldn't understand the statement that "even if pitch and volume change, the shape of the sound wave stays the same." Other students agreed that the information about pitch and volume was particularly difficult to understand, but some of them tried to help clarify it. Collin began to understand the concept a little better, but he admitted it was still fuzzy in his mind. Finally, Collin examined the list of topics along the side of the page from the

FIGURE 3.10
Reciprocal Teaching

Summarizing—After students have silently or orally read a short section of a passage, a single student acting as teacher (i.e., the student leader) summarizes what has been read. Other students, with guidance from the teacher, may add to the summary. If students have difficulty summarizing, the teacher might point out clues (e.g., important items or obvious topic sentences) that aid in the construction of good summaries.

Questioning—The student leader asks some questions to which the class responds. The questions are designed to help students identify important information in the passage. For example, the student leader might look back over the selection and ask questions about specific pieces of information. The other students then try to answer these questions, based on their recollection of the information.

Clarifying—Next, the student leader tries to clarify confusing points in the passage. He might point these out or ask other students to point them out. For example, the student leader might say, "The part about why the dog ran into the car was confusing to me. Can anyone explain this?" Or, the student leader might ask students to ask clarification questions. The group then attempts to clear up the confusing parts. This might involve rereading parts of the passage.

Predicting—The student leader asks for predictions about what will happen in the next segment of the text. The leader can write the predictions on the blackboard or on an overhead, or all students can write them down in their notebooks.

Web site, and predicted that they were now going to learn about tone, harmonics, sound waves, and frequencies as they are applied to the brass, string, percussion, and woodwind instruments.

Research and Theory on Note Taking

Note taking is closely related to summarizing. To take effective notes, a student must make a determination as to what is most important, and then state that information in a parsimonious form. As we have seen, this is at the heart of summarizing. Researchers have conducted many studies on the effects of note taking on student achievement. Figure 3.11 shows the results of some of these studies.

A useful source for a review of many of these studies is the monograph entitled *Note-Taking: What Do We Know About the Benefits?* (Beecher, 1988). We have found several generalizations drawn from the research that can be used to guide instruction on note taking.

1. **Verbatim note taking is, perhaps, the least effective way to take notes.** A fair amount of research supports the intuitive perception that verbatim note taking is not an effective strategy (see Bretzing & Kulhary, 1979). It is probably true that when students are trying to record everything they hear or read, they are not engaged in the act of synthesizing information. Trying to record all of what is heard or read takes up so much of a student's working memory

FIGURE 3.11

Research Results for Note Taking

Synthesis Study	No. of Effect Sizes (ESs)	Ave. ES	Percentile Gain
Henk & Stahl, 1985[a]	25	.34	13
	11	1.56	44
Marzano, Gnadt, & Jesse, 1990	3	1.26	40
Hattie et al., 1996	3	1.05	35
Ganske, 1981	24	.52	20

[a] Two categories of effect sizes are listed for the Henk and Stahl study because of the manner in which the effect sizes were reported. Readers should consult that study for more details.

that she does not have "room" to analyze the incoming information.

2. **Notes should be considered a work in progress.** Once students initially take notes, teachers should encourage them to continually add to the notes and revise them as their understanding of content deepens and sharpens (for discussions, see Anderson, T. H., & Armbruster, 1986; Denner, 1986; Einstein, Morris, & Smith, 1985). This implies that teachers should systematically provide time for students to go back over their notes—reviewing and revising them. The review-and-revision process can be a particularly powerful activity if encouraged and directed by the teacher. Specifically, a teacher might help students identify and correct misconceptions in notes they have previously taken.

3. **Notes should be used as study guides for tests.** One of the more practical uses of notes is as test preparation tools. If notes have been well designed and students have systematically elaborated on them, they can provide a powerful form of review for students (for discussions, see Carrier & Titus, 1981; Carter & Van Matre, 1975; Van Matre & Carter, 1975). Interestingly, fewer students than might be expected take advantage of notes to this end. This might be because they are simply unaware of this potentially powerful use of notes, or they do not know how to structure their time to adequately prepare for tests using their notes.

4. **The more notes that are taken, the better.** One of the common misconceptions about note taking is that "less is more." That is, sometimes students are advised to keep their notes very short. Indeed, researchers Nye, Crooks, Powlie, and Tripp (1984) explain that in their examination of study guides prepared by universities to teach students how to take notes, "Five out of ten

guides examined emphasized the importance of keeping notes 'brief' and not putting too much material in notes" (p. 95). Yet, in their study of the effects of note taking, Nye et al. found that there was a strong relationship between the amount of information taken in notes and students' achievement on examinations.

Classroom Practice in Note Taking

Teacher-Prepared Notes

Teacher-prepared notes (Figure 3.12) are one of the most straightforward uses of

---

FIGURE 3.12

Teacher-Prepared Notes: The Bill of Rights

I. **What It Is**
   The Bill of Rights is the first 10 amendments to the U.S. Constitution. It protects fundamental individual rights and liberties.

II. **The History of the Bill of Rights**
   A. James Madison, congressman from Virginia, proposed a series of amendments to the Constitution. Madison introduced these amendments in the House of Representatives in May, 1789.
   B. Committees of the House of Representatives and the Senate rewrote the amendments.
   C. The House and Senate approved 12 amendments in September, 1789.
   D. Ten of the 12 proposed amendments were ratified on December 14, 1791.
      1. "Ratification" is the name of the process by which constitutional amendments are approved. To be adopted, an amendment must be passed by two-thirds of each house of Congress and then by three-fourths of the state legislatures.
      2. The state legislatures voted on each of the 12 amendments separately. The first 2 proposed amendments were not ratified by three-quarters of the states.

III. **Rights Protected by the Bill of Rights**
   A. More than 30 liberties and rights are protected by the 10 amendments that make up the Bill of Rights.
   B. Each amendment protects specific rights:
      1. Protects freedom of speech, press, assembly, and religious belief; prohibits the government from creating a state religion or giving support to any or all religions.
      2. Protects the right to bear arms.
      3. Prohibits the government, even the military, from invading our homes.
      4. Prohibits unreasonable searches and arrests; declares that there must be probable cause for a search or arrest warrant to be issued.
      5. Prohibits double jeopardy; protects right to remain silent; prohibits government from taking away anyone's life, liberty, or property without due process of law.
      6. Protects right to a fair trial, including right to be represented by counsel in a speedy trial before an impartial jury.
      7. Protects right to trial by jury; prohibits courts from reexamining facts tried by a jury.
      8. Prohibits excessive bail or fines, or the infliction of cruel and unusual punishment.
      9. Preserves any individual rights or liberties not specifically mentioned in the Constitution.
      10. Preserves the power of the states

notes. First, these notes provide students with a clear picture of what the teacher considers important. Second, they provide students with a model of how notes might be taken. The example in Figure 3.12 shows a few notes a teacher might give students for the topic of the Bill of Rights.

Formats for Notes

There is no one correct way to take notes. In fact, different students might prefer different note-taking formats. Consequently,

it is advisable to present students with a variety of formats. One common format is the *informal outline*. The informal outline uses indentation to indicate major ideas and their related details. Figure 3.13 depicts notes generated by a student on the topic of blood. The student has simply indented ideas that are more subordinate in nature.

Webbing is a note-taking strategy that uses the relative size of circles to indicate the importance of ideas and lines to indicate relationships. The more important ideas have larger circles than the less impor-

---

FIGURE 3.13

Student Notes: Informal Outline

The Circulatory System

One of the transport systems of the body
   3 functions:
      carries food and oxygen to cells
      carries away wastes from cells
      protects the body from disease
   3 parts:
      heart
      blood vessels
      blood

One of the parts of the circulatory system is blood
   4 parts:
      plasma
      red blood cells
      white blood cells
      platelets

   The liquid part of the blood—plasma
      yellowish in color and mostly water
      contains food and wastes
      makes up over half of the blood

One of the solid parts of the blood is the red blood cells
   pick up oxygen in the lungs and carry it to cells

pick up carbon dioxide from the cells and carry it to the lungs
shaped like a doughnut without the hole—is very small.
contains hemoglobin to help it do its job
about 5 million red blood cells in one drop of blood

Second solid part of the blood is white blood cells
   help the body fight infection
   have no color and change shape as they move
   fight infection by surrounding bacteria and digesting it

Third solid part of the blood is platelets
   stop bleeding by causing blood to thicken and clot
   not whole cells, but parts of cells
   have no color and are smaller than red blood cells

Hemoglobin is a chemical in red blood cells
   contains iron
   makes the color of red blood cells
   helps the red blood cells transport materials to and from cells

tant ideas. Lines from one circle to another indicate that the concepts in the connected circles are related in some way. One advantage of the webbing format is that it provides a visual representation of the information. One disadvantage of the webbing strategy is that it somewhat limits the amount of information a student can record simply because the circles themselves can hold only so much verbiage. Figure 3.14 portrays webbed notes for the topic of the Olympic games.

Combination Notes

One flexible note-taking strategy employs both the informal outline and the web formats. It might be referred to as a combination technique. With this strategy, each page of notes is divided into three parts by a line running down the middle of the page and a horizontal line near the bottom of the page. The left-hand side of the page is reserved for notes taken using informal outlining or a variation of it. The right-

FIGURE 3.14

Student Notes: Webbing

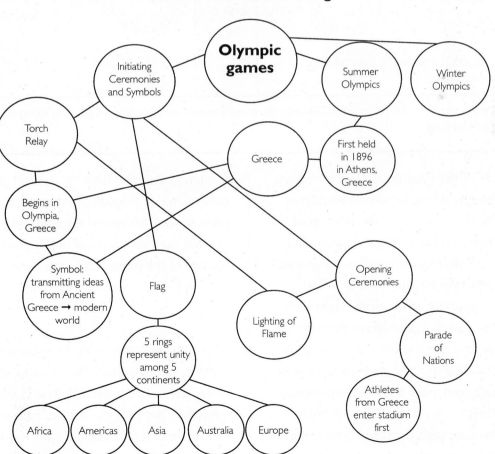

FIGURE 3.15

Student Notes: Combination Technique

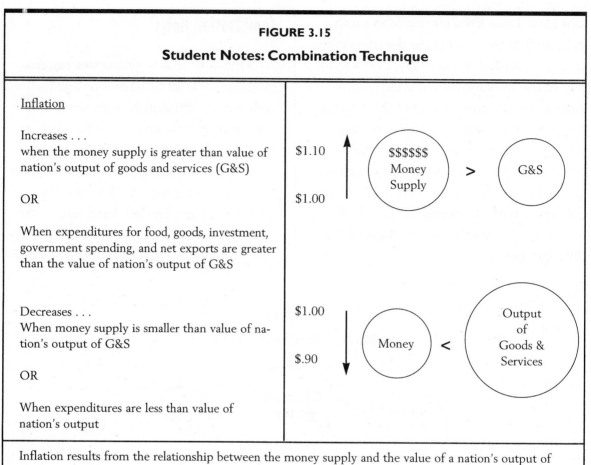

Inflation

Increases . . .
when the money supply is greater than value of nation's output of goods and services (G&S)

OR

When expenditures for food, goods, investment, government spending, and net exports are greater than the value of nation's output of G&S

Decreases . . .
When money supply is smaller than value of nation's output of G&S

OR

When expenditures are less than value of nation's output

$1.10

$1.00

$$$$$$
Money Supply > G&S

$1.00

$.90

Money < Output of Goods & Services

Inflation results from the relationship between the money supply and the value of a nation's output of goods and services.

hand side of the page is reserved for notes taken using webbing or some variation of it. Finally, the strip across the bottom of the page is reserved for summary statements. Figure 3.15 shows combination notes a student might take for the topic of inflation.

The important aspect of the right-hand side of the page is that students portray the information in some visual way. To employ this note-taking strategy, students must stop periodically and make a graphic representation of their notes on the right side of the page. This note-taking method takes extra time but forces students to consider the in-

formation a second time. At the end of their note taking, or periodically throughout the process, students record summary statements of what they have learned in the space at the bottom of the page. This forces them to process the information a third time.

♦ ♦ ♦

Although we sometimes refer to summarizing and note taking as mere "study skills," they are two of the most powerful skills students can cultivate. They provide students with tools for identifying and understanding the most important aspects of what they are learning.

4

REINFORCING EFFORT AND PROVIDING RECOGNITION

Ian MacIntosh was a new student at Prairie Elementary School. It did not take him long to discover that even though the teachers and students seemed nice enough, the school was considered to be what they called a "low-performing school." They had low scores on the state tests, and everyone knew it because the results were published in the local newspaper. The test was given soon after Ian arrived and, like other students, he just wanted to get through it.

The next year, the school got a new principal, Ms. Heichman. Things began to change. Ian's teachers started telling stories of famous people who achieved their goals because they believed that if they tried hard enough, they could do anything. Even students were asked to give examples, and Ian told the story of his grandfather's belief that he could make his farm successful. Ian's teachers started giving students "E for Effort" certificates. Ian earned two in one week. It made him feel more confident and made him want to do better. His classmates all seemed a bit more confident, too, especially when the whole class received the principal's "E for Effort" award because the class beat their own previous class average on math quizzes, twice in one month. He was proud when the banner went up over the door—and he enjoyed the ice cream the room mothers had promised them if they hit their goal.

The best news came when the state test scores returned. The school was in the headlines as the school that had improved the most. Ian knew he and his schoolmates still had a long way to go, but he believed they could do it.

The approach used by Ian's principal exemplifies the third category of general instructional strategies. Unlike the others, it does not deal directly with enhancing or engaging the cognitive skills of students. Rather, this set of instructional techniques addresses students' attitudes and beliefs. This category has been subdivided into two parts: reinforcing effort and providing recognition.

Research and Theory on Reinforcing Effort

It was probably psychologist Bernard Weiner (1972, 1983) who popularized the notion that a belief in effort ultimately pays off in terms of enhanced achievement. Research by Covington (1983) and Harter (1980) has also shown the effect of believing in the importance of effort. More specifically, this body of research demonstrates that people generally attribute success at any given task to one of four causes:

+ Ability
+ Effort
+ Other people
+ Luck

Three of these four beliefs ultimately inhibit achievement. On the surface, a belief in ability seems relatively useful—if you believe you have ability, you can tackle anything. Regardless of how much ability you think you have, however, there will inevitably be tasks for which you do not believe you have the requisite skill. In fact, Covington's research (1983, 1985) indicates that a belief on the part of students that they do not possess the necessary ability to succeed at a task might cause them to sabotage their own success. Belief that

other people are the primary cause of success also has drawbacks, particularly when an individual finds himself or herself alone. Belief in luck has obvious disadvantages—what if your luck runs out? Belief in effort is clearly the most useful attribution. If you believe that effort is the most important factor in achievement, you have a motivational tool that can apply to any situation.

Several researchers have attempted to synthesize the studies on the effects on student achievement of reinforcing effort. Figure 4.1 shows the results from some of those syntheses.

We have drawn two generalizations from the research on effort:

1. **Not all students realize the importance of believing in effort.** Although it might seem obvious to adults—particularly successful ones—that effort pays off in terms of enhanced achievement, not all students are aware of this. In fact, studies have demonstrated that some students are not aware of the fact that the effort they put into a task has a direct effect on their success relative to the task (see Seligman, 1990, 1994; Urdan, Midgley, & Anderman, 1998). The implication here is that teachers should explain and exemplify the "effort belief" to students.

2. **Students can learn to change their beliefs to an emphasis on effort.** Probably, one of the most promising aspects of the research on effort is that students can learn to operate from a belief that effort pays off even if they do not initially have this belief.

FIGURE 4.1

Research Results for Reinforcing Effort

Synthesis Study	No. of Effect Sizes (ESs)	Ave. ES	Percentile Gain
Schunk & Cox, 1986	3	.93	32
Stipek & Weisz, 1981[a]	98	.52	20
Hattie, Biggs, & Purdie, 1996[b]	8	1.42	42
	2	.57	22
	2	2.14	48
Kumar, 1991	5	1.76	46

[a] These studies also dealt with students' sense of control.
[b] Multiple categories of effect sizes are listed for the Hattie et al. study because of the manner in which effect size was reported. Readers should consult that study for more details.

An interesting set of studies has shown that simply demonstrating that added effort will pay off in terms of enhanced achievement actually increases student achievement (see Craske, 1985; Wilson & Linville, 1982). In fact, one study (Van Overwalle & De Metsenaere, 1990) found that students who were taught about the relationship between effort and achievement increased their achievement more than students who were taught techniques for time management and comprehension of new material.

Classroom Practice in Reinforcing Effort

Teaching About Effort

The preceding generalizations, taken together, assert that students might not be aware of the importance of believing in effort, but they can be taught. The remedy for this is for teachers to make sure that they explicitly teach and exemplify the connection between effort and achievement. For example, teachers might share personal examples of times that they succeeded by continuing to try even when success did not appear imminent. Teachers might also seek out and share examples of well-known athletes, educators, and political or social leaders who succeeded in large part simply because they didn't give up (e.g., Daniel "Rudy" Ruettiger, the Notre Dame student whose unwavering commitment to play on the university's football team was the subject of the inspiring movie *Rudy*). Examples might also be shared from stories that are familiar to students (e.g., *The Little Engine That Could*). Still another way to help students understand the value of effort is to ask them to recall personal examples of times that they succeeded primarily because they didn't give up. The following example shows how a teacher reinforced the effort attribution in the context of the Olympic games.

> For an entire week, the students in a high school general math class were given no math homework. Rather, their assignment each night was to watch the Winter Olympics, paying particular attention to the "up close and personal" stories about specific athletes. The students were to look for examples of ordinary people who achieved extraordinary things because they believed that sustained effort would lead to achievement of their goals. The first five minutes of each class period that week were used to let students discuss, in small groups and as a whole class, the stories they had heard and the different strategies that the athletes used to keep believing in themselves. By Monday of the next week, each student was to come

up with a way to remind themselves to keep trying when things got difficult in class.

Keeping Track of Effort and Achievement

The generalizations in this category suggest how important it is for students to understand the relationship between effort and achievement. Teaching *about* effort, as suggested previously, might work for some students, but others will need to see the connection between effort and achievement for themselves. A powerful way to help them make this connection is to ask students to periodically keep track of their effort and its relationship to achievement. This can be accomplished by presenting them with rubrics like those shown in Figure 4.2 (A and B).

FIGURE 4.2

Effort and Achievement Rubrics

Scale: 4 = excellent; 3 = good; 2 = needs improvement; 1 = unacceptable

A: Effort Rubric

4   I worked on the task until it was completed. I pushed myself to continue working on the task even when difficulties arose or a solution was not immediately evident. I viewed difficulties that arose as opportunities to strengthen my understanding.

3   I worked on the task until it was completed. I pushed myself to continue working on the task even when difficulties arose or a solution was not immediately evident.

2   I put some effort into the task, but I stopped working when difficulties arose.

1   I put very little effort into the task.

B: Achievement Rubric

4   I exceeded the objectives of the task or lesson.

3   I met the objectives of the task or lesson.

2   I met a few of the objectives of the task or lesson, but did not meet others.

1   I did not meet the objectives of the task or lesson.

FIGURE 4.3

Effort and Achievement Chart

Student _____	Assignment	Effort Rubric	Achievement Rubric
Fri., Oct. 22	Homework—5-paragraph essay re: *Animal Farm*	4	4
Wed., Oct. 27	In-class essay re: allegory	4	3
Thurs., Oct. 28	Pop quiz	3	3

Students might use these rubrics to keep track of their effort and achievement on a daily basis for a week. To do this, a teacher would have students record the relationship between their effort and achievement in a table like that in Figure 4.3.

In addition to charting the relationship between the two variables, students might be asked to identify what they learned from the experience. Reflecting on their experiences and then verbalizing what they learned can help students heighten their awareness of the power of effort. The following example describes how this technique was used in a particular class:

Jane Whitby was accustomed to being asked to keep a learning log in the back of her notebook. She dutifully compiled notes in her log book when asked to write about what she was learning and how well she had learned it. One day in March, a time when it was almost always difficult for her to be enthusiastic about school, her teacher gave the learning log a different spin. Students were each given a piece of graph paper and were shown how to create a line graph to chart their learning and their effort. The horizontal axis was to be labeled with the days of the week, spanning two full weeks. The vertical axis was to represent percentages from 1 to 100. For two weeks, each day, students plotted the relationship between their level of effort (1–100 percent) and how they rated their level of learning (percent of what they could have learned). At the end of the two weeks, Jane and her classmates noticed that this graph actually motivated them; many admitted that when they felt like just "coasting," the picture of the graph popped into their heads.

Research and Theory on Providing Recognition

"Providing Recognition," as a category of instructional strategies, might be the most misunderstood of all those presented in this book. Another name for this category might have been "praise"—although that would be technically inaccurate. Still, another name for this category might have been "reward"—although that, too, would be technically inaccurate. For reasons explained subsequently, we prefer to use the term *recognition*. Figure 4.4 shows results from studies that have attempted to synthesize the research on recognition.

FIGURE 4.4

Research Results for Providing Recognition

Synthesis Study	No. of Effect Sizes (ESs)	Ave. ES	Percentile Gain
Bloom, 1976	18	.78	28
Walberg, 1999	14	.16	6
Wilkinson, 1981	791	.16	7

Figure 4.4 doesn't paint a very flattering picture of the effectiveness of this activity, especially the finding in the Walberg (1999) and Wilkinson (1981) studies. But the studies summarized in the figure primarily addressed the use of *praise* as recognition. It is probably because of results like these that many educators believe that any form of recognition not only doesn't enhance student achievement, but decreases intrinsic motivation. Given the misunderstanding surrounding this area, we should briefly consider the history of the research on praise and reward as forms of recognition.

The first laboratory investigations of the effects of reward on intrinsic motivation were conducted by researcher Deci (1971). In the first experiment, 24 college students were randomly assigned to one of two groups. Both groups were assigned problems to solve. The experimental group was paid $1 for each correctly answered problem. Students' "intrinsic" motivation for the task was measured by counting the number of times they engaged in the puzzle-solving task during their free time. Deci found that students in the group that were paid, spent significantly less time on the puzzles during free time than did the experimental group. Deci commented:

> If a person is engaged in some activity for reasons of intrinsic motivation and if he begins to receive the external reward, money, for performing the activity, the degree to which he is intrinsically motivated to perform the activity decreases (Deci, 1971, p. 108).

This finding was taken by some as evidence that rewards, in general, decrease intrinsic motivation (see Kohn, 1993). Another study commonly cited as evidence that rewards of all types diminish intrinsic motivation, is that conducted by researchers Lepper, Greene, and Nisbett (1973). Their study examined the effect of rewards on the intrinsic motivation of young children to draw. The reward for the experimental group was to be given a "good player" award if they drew pictures. Again, it was concluded that external reward decreased motivation.

Much of the research on teacher praise has also contributed to the perception that recognition decreases intrinsic motivation (for reviews see Brophy, 1981; Lepper,

1983; Morine-Dershimer, 1982). For example, it appears that praise given for accomplishing easy tasks can undermine achievement. Students commonly perceived it as undeserved; further, praise for accomplishing easy tasks might actually lower their perception of their ability (Morine-Dershimer).

It also seems that praise is commonly handed out unsystematically and unevenly by teachers. One study found that first-grade teachers praised only about 11 percent of students' correct responses (see Anderson, L., Evertson, & Brophy, 1979). Another study found that junior high school teachers praised only about 10 percent of students' correct responses (see Evertson, Anderson, Anderson, & Brophy, 1980). Researcher Jere Brophy (1981) summarized the guidelines for effective praise (see Figure 4.5).

If we were to take the preceding discussion at face value, it would be fairly easy to conclude that providing praise or rewards in any form not only doesn't enhance achievement, but it also is detrimental to motivation. However, a thorough review of the research provides a very different picture. There are three generalizations that can be extracted from the research.

1. Rewards do not necessarily have a negative effect on intrinsic motivation. Those who have carefully analyzed all the research on rewards, commonly came to the conclusion that they do not necessarily decrease intrinsic motivation. For example,

in his review of the research on rewards, Mark Morgan (1984) concluded: "The central finding emerging from the present review is that rewards can have either undermining or enhancing effects depending on circumstance" (p. 25). Major meta-analyses conducted by Wiersma (1992) and by Cameron and Pierce (1994) have provided a strong research base for this conclusion. To illustrate, consider the findings reported in Figure 4.6 (see p. 57).

Figure 4.6 rather dramatically illustrates the fact that depending on how researchers measure intrinsic motivation, they can come up with different conclusions. Specifically, when intrinsic motivation is measured using students' *free-time* activity—whether they engage in the activity during time when they are not asked to—the results of 44 studies show a slightly negative effect on intrinsic motivation of –.04. When intrinsic motivation is measured by examining student *attitudes* toward the activity, however, 39 studies indicate that rewards positively affect intrinsic motivation, and have an effect size of .14. Finally, when students' ability to perform the "rewarded" activity is examined, 11 studies indicate that rewards have a positive effect of .34. In short, the research indicates that rewards have a negative effect on intrinsic motivation "only when intrinsic motivation is operationalized as task behavior during a free time measure" (Wiersma, 1992, p. 101).

2. Reward is most effective when it is contingent on the attainment of some stan-

FIGURE 4.5

Guidelines for Effective Praise

Effective Praise ...	Ineffective Praise ...
1. Is delivered contingently.	1. Is delivered randomly or unsystematically.
2. Specifies the particulars of the accomplishment.	2. Is restricted to global positive reactions.
3. Shows spontaneity, variety, and other signs of credibility; suggests clear attention to the students' accomplishments.	3. Shows a bland uniformity that suggests a conditional response made with minimal attention.
4. Rewards attainment of specified performance criteria (which can include effort criteria).	4. Rewards mere participation, without consideration of performance, processes, or outcomes.
5. Provides information to students about their competence or the value of their accomplishments.	5. Provides no information at all or gives students no information about their status.
6. Orients students toward better appreciation of their own task-related behavior and thinking about problem solving.	6. Orients students toward comparing themselves with others and thinking about competing.
7. Uses students' own prior accomplishments as the context for describing present accomplishments.	7. Uses the accomplishments of peers as the context for describing students' present accomplishments.
8. Is given in recognition of noteworthy effort or success at difficult (for this student) tasks.	8. Is given without regard to the effort expended or the meaning of the accomplishment.
9. Attributes success to effort and ability, implying that similar successes can be expected in the future.	9. Attributes success to ability alone or to external factors such as luck or low task difficulty.
10. Fosters endogenous attributions (students believe that they expend effort on the task because they enjoy the task and/or want to develop task-relevant skills).	10. Fosters exogenous attributions (students believe that they expend effort on the task for external reasons — to please the teacher, win a competition or reward, etc.).
11. Focuses students' attention on their own task-relevant behavior.	11. Focuses students' attention on the teacher as an external authority who is manipulating them.
12. Fosters appreciation of, and desirable attributions about, task-relevant behavior after the process is completed.	12. Intrudes into the ongoing process, distracting attention from task-relevant behavior.

Source: Brophy, J. (1981). Teacher praise: A functional analysis. *Review of Educational Research, 51,* 5–32. Adapted by permission.

dard of performance. The meta-analyses by Wiersma (1992) and by Cameron and Pierce (1994) both provide strong support for the generalization that reward works fairly well when it is based on the attainment of some performance standards. In fact, nine separate studies in the Wiersma meta-analyses, considered as a group, indicate that the average effect size for reward

used in this way is .38. Findings similar to these led Cameron and Pierce to note:

> Rewards can have a negative impact on intrinsic motivation when they are offered to people for engaging in a task without considering any standard of performance. In a classroom, this might occur if a teacher promised students tangible rewards simply for doing an activity. [However], this would not occur if the teacher used the same re-

FIGURE 4.6

Meta-analytic Results Supporting Rewards

Study	Measure Used to Assess Intrinsic Motivation	No. of Effect Sizes (ESs)	Average ES	Percentile Gain
Cameron & Pierce, 1994	Free time	44	–.04	–2
	Attitude	39	.14	6
Wiersma, 1992	Performance	11	.34	13

wards but made this contingent on successful completion of the problems. (p. 397)

Stated differently, rewarding students for simply performing a task does not enhance intrinsic motivation and might even decrease it. This is probably so because it conveys the message that students must be "paid off" to engage in the activity. Providing rewards for the successful attainment of specific performance goals, however, enhances intrinsic motivation.

3. **Abstract symbolic recognition is more effective than tangible rewards.** The final generalization about recognition is that, abstract, symbolic recognition is more effective than tangible rewards. This is an important distinction. Many of the studies that produced negative results for the use of rewards, used tangible rewards such as money and candy. We should first note that even these tangible rewards can have a positive effect on intrinsic motivation when they are used in accordance with Generalization 2—as contingent on the completion of some performance standard. The research

indicates, however, that the more abstract and symbolic forms of reward are, the more powerful they are. To illustrate, consider the findings in Figure 4.7, which are taken from the study by Cameron and Pierce (1994).

Notice that the use of verbal rewards has effect sizes of .42 and .45 on intrinsic motivation when motivation is measured by attitude and free time, respectively—verbal reward seems to work no matter how one measures intrinsic motivation. Tangible rewards, on the other hand, do not seem to work well as motivators, regardless of how motivation is measured. These powerful findings for verbal recognition led researchers Cameron and Pierce to note:

When praise and other forms of positive feedback are given and later removed, people continued to show interest in their work. In contrast to recent claims made by Kohn (1993, p. 55), verbal praise is an extrinsic motivator that positively alters attitude and behaviors (1994, p. 397).

Given the validity of the three generalizations above, it appears obvious that abstract

FIGURE 4.7

Influence of Abstract Versus Tangible Rewards

Type of Reward	No. of Effect Sizes (ESs)	Ave. ES	Percentile Gain
Verbal on attitude	15	.42	16
Verbal on free time	15	.45	17
Tangible on attitude	37	.04	2
Tangible on free time	51	−.20	−8

*Computed from data in Cameron and Pierce, 1994.

rewards—particularly praise—when given for accomplishing specific performance goals, can be a powerful motivator for students. Given the lack of understanding of the effects of these types of rewards and the negative opinion some educators have adopted toward them, we believe that the best way to think of abstract contingency-based rewards is as "recognition"—recognition for specific accomplishments. This is why we have entitled this section "recognition" as opposed to "reward" or "praise."

Classroom Practice in Providing Recognition

Personalizing Recognition

When recognizing the accomplishment of a performance standard as articulated in Generalization 2, it is best to make this recognition as personal to the students as possible. The following example describes the efforts of a group of teachers to estab-

lish school routines that result in personalizing recognition for students.

At a high school faculty meeting, teachers were engaged in a lively conversation about grading practices. Some teachers made the case that a significant number of students were making major improvements in their academic work, but might never make the honor role. Although some teachers argued that "that's the way real life is," others countered by reiterating the mission of the school—"to help all students reach their potential." As a result of this conversation, and because of the work of a designated task force, the school developed a program where students—at all achievement levels—were helped to set ambitious personal achievement goals. Anyone who achieved his or her goal was recognized publicly by making the "Personal Best" Honor Role. This evolved into an honor as coveted as much as, if not more than, making the traditional honor role.

Pause, Prompt, and Praise

One strategy that makes effective use of praise is an adaptation of what is commonly referred to as "Pause, Prompt, and

Praise" (see Merrett & Thorpe, 1996). This strategy is best used while students are engaged in a particularly demanding task with which they are having difficulty. During the "pause" phase of the strategy, the teacher asks the students to stop working on the task for a moment. During that time, teacher and student have a brief discussion as to why the student is experiencing difficulty. As a "prompt," the teacher provides the student with some specific suggestion for improving his or her performance. If the student's performance improves as a result of implementing this suggestion, then "praise" is given. The following example depicts the potential positive influence of this strategy in a math class.

> Jake was struggling with long division and was becoming discouraged. His frustration must have been obvious because the teacher stopped at his desk and asked him to put down his pencil. When she saw that he was making mistakes mainly because his columns were sloppy, she gave him a piece of graph paper and showed him how to use it to make sure his numbers were lined up properly. He was surprised how well it worked and was thrilled when the next time the teacher stopped at his desk, it was to congratulate him on having completed four problems with no mistakes.

Concrete Symbols of Recognition

Many teachers, who consistently give appropriate verbal recognition for their students' accomplishments, would agree that it is also appropriate to offer their students concrete, symbolic tokens of recognition.

Stickers, awards, coupons, and treats are examples of the types of tokens that are commonly used. As stated in the first generalization in this chapter, these tokens do not necessarily diminish the intrinsic motivation if the tokens are given for accomplishing specific performance goals. The following example illustrates the use of concrete tokens in an informal but effective way.

> Darryl had been in the International Baccalaureate program for two years. He loved to learn and was generally successful, but, for some reason, he was feeling burned out this semester. His grades had slipped a little, and his mind was wandering in class. His teacher noticed this. She saw similar symptoms in other students. Fortunately for Darryl, she decided that her "serious" students, like Darryl, needed to lighten up. During the two weeks leading up to a particularly important exam, she systematically gave short practice quizzes. Every time a student scored between 90 and 100 percent, or scored 10 points higher than the previous day, he or she received a prize. The prizes? Smiley face stickers, McDonald's toys, cracker jacks, paper party hats. Darryl and his classmates got into it. Cheers and laughter accompanied every awards ceremony. More important, when the teacher announced the scores for the big examination, academic performance had never been better.

◆ ◆ ◆

Reinforcing effort can help teach students one of the most valuable lessons they can learn—the harder you try, the more successful you are. In addition, providing recognition for attainment of specific goals not only enhances achievement, but it stimulates motivation.

5

HOMEWORK AND PRACTICE

"I hate homework. Why can't we just learn at school and be done with it? I know how to do these problems, and I've shown that I understand them. So, why do I have to do 25?" Jeff had expressed this point of view many times before, but this time his mother had an answer.

"At Back-to-School night, your teachers explained some things about homework to us and went over what they see as the parent's job. Let me see if I get this right. If they asked you to do 25 problems, you are probably supposed to practice in order to increase your accuracy and speed. So it's probably not a good idea to sit there in front of the TV while you do the problems."

Jeff's mother also remembered some of the tips the parents were given for helping students with their homework. "OK. Here is the kitchen timer. When I say 'Go,' do the first five problems and yell 'Stop' when you finish." For the next 30 minutes, Jeff charted and tried to beat his time as he did each set of 5 problems, making sure that he also attended to being accurate. He had to admit that the time flew by and that it was kind of fun.

"Your teacher will love it if you hand in your chart with the completed problems," Jeff's mom suggested. In fact, Jeff's teacher liked it so much that the students' speed and accuracy charts became the focus of the teacher's feedback whenever the goal was to practice a skill.

Homework and practice are instructional techniques that are well known to teachers. Both provide students with opportunities to deepen their understanding and skills relative to content that has been initially presented to them.

60

Research and Theory on Homework

It is no exaggeration to say that homework is a staple of U.S. education. By the time students reach the middle grades, homework has become a part of their lives. The reason commonly cited for homework makes good sense: It extends learning opportunities beyond the confines of the school day. This might be necessary because "schooling occupies only about 13 percent of the waking hours of the first 18 years of life," which is less than the amount of time students spend watching television (Fraser, Walberg, Welch, & Hattie, 1987, p. 234). Figure 5.1 shows some of the research findings on homework.

We have found four generalizations that can guide teachers in the use of homework.

1. The amount of homework assigned to students should be different from ele- mentary to middle school to high school. One of the controversies surrounding homework is whether it is an effective learning tool for students at the elementary level. This first became an issue as a result of the findings of a meta-analysis conducted by researcher Harris Cooper (1989 a, b). After a review of the research up to 1988, Cooper reported the following effect sizes:

Grades 4–6:	ES = .15
Grades 7–9:	ES = .31
Grades 10–12:	ES = .64

Whereas homework in high school produces a gain of about 24 percentile points, homework in the middle grades produces a gain of only 12 percentile points. What was most striking in Cooper's finding is that homework had a relatively small effect—a percentile gain of 6 points—on student achievement at grades 4–6. This finding has led some to conclude that elementary students should not be assigned any home-

FIGURE 5.1				
Research Results for Homework				
Synthesis Study	**Focus**	**No. of Effect Sizes (ESs)**	**Ave. ES**	**Percentile Gain**
Paschal, Weinstein, & Walberg, 1984	General effects of homework	81	.36	14
Graue, Weinstein, & Walberg, 1983	General effects of homework	29	.49	19
Hattie, 1992	General effects of homework	110	.43	1
Ross, 1988	General effects of homework	53	.65	24

work. It is important to note that since Cooper's meta-analysis, there have been a number of studies (some of them conducted by Cooper) indicating that homework does produce beneficial results for students in grades as low as 2nd grade (see Cooper, Lindsay, Nye, & Greathouse, 1998; Cooper, Valentine, Nye, & Lindsay, 1999; Good, Grouws, & Ebmeier, 1983; Gorges & Elliott, 1995; Rosenberg, 1989). In fact, even though Cooper found little effect for homework for students at the elementary level in his 1989 (a and b) report, he still recommended homework for elementary students:

> First, I recommend that elementary students be given homework even though it should not be expected to improve test scores. Instead, homework for young children should help them develop good study habits, foster positive attitudes toward school, and communicate to students the idea that learning takes work at home as well as at school (1989b, p. 90).

Given the findings in recent years that homework does positively influence the achievement of elementary students and the 1989 (a and b) endorsement by Cooper, even though his synthesis of the research at that time did not show a relationship between elementary school homework and achievement, it is safe to conclude that students in grades from, at least 2nd and beyond, should be asked to do *some* homework.

This said, it is also important to realize that students at lower grade levels should be given far less homework than students at higher grade levels. The critical question is how much homework is the *right amount* of homework. Unfortunately, there is no clear answer on this point. Figure 5.2 presents recommendations from various studies.

FIGURE 5.2
Recommended Total Minutes Per Day for Homework

Grade Level	Pennsylvania Dept. of Education, 1973	Leone & Richard, 1989	Bond & Smith, 1966	Strang, 1975	Keith, 1982	Tymms & Fitz-Gibbs, 1992
Primary	30		20–29	10		
Upper Elementary	45–90		30–40	40*		
Middle School / Jr. High School	90–120	50	50	60*		
High School	120–180			120	60*	60

* These numbers are estimates, based on the author's comments.

Finally, even though there is certainly a practical (and ethical) limit to the amount of homework that should be assigned to students at the high school level, the more homework students do, the better their achievement. Specifically, Keith's data indicate that for about every 30 minutes of "additional" homework a student does per night, his or her overall grade point average (GPA) increases about half a point. This means that if a student with a GPA of 2.00 increases the amount of homework she does by 30 minutes per night, her GPA will rise to 2.50.

2. Parent involvement in homework should be kept to a minimum. It is probably safe to say that many parents assume that they should help their children with homework. In fact, some districts have written homework policies articulating how parents should be involved (Roderique, Pulloway, Cumblad, & Epstein, 1994). While it is certainly legitimate to inform parents of the homework assigned to their children, it does not seem advisable to have parents help their children with homework. Specifically, many studies show minimal and even somewhat negative effects when parents are asked to help students with homework (see Balli, 1998; Balli, Demo, & Wedman, 1998; Balli, Wedman, & Demo, 1997; Perkins & Milgram, 1996). This does not mean that parents should not help "facilitate" homework, as demonstrated by Jeff's mother in the vignette introducing this chapter. Parents

should be careful, however, not to solve content problems for students.

3. The purpose of homework should be identified and articulated. Not all homework is the same. That is, homework can be assigned for different purposes, and depending on the purpose, the form of homework and the feedback provided students will differ. Two common purposes for homework are (1) practice and (2) preparation or elaboration (see Foyle, 1985; Foyle & Bailey, 1988; Foyle, Lyman, Tompkins, Perne, & Foyle, 1990). When homework is assigned for the purpose of practice, it should be structured around content with which students have a high degree of familiarity. For example, if students are asked to practice a new skill they have learned in class via homework, they should be fairly familiar with that skill. Practicing a skill with which a student is unfamiliar is not only inefficient, but might also serve to habituate errors or misconceptions.

A second general purpose for homework is to prepare students for new content or have them elaborate on content that has been introduced. For example, a teacher might assign homework to have students begin thinking about the concept of the cell prior to systematically studying it in class. Similarly, after that concept of the cell has been introduced, the teacher might assign homework that asks students to elaborate on what they have learned. In both of these situations, it is not necessary that students have an in-depth understanding of the content (as is the case when homework is used for practice).

4. If homework is assigned, it should be commented on. One set of studies (see Walberg, 1999) found that the effects of homework vary greatly, depending on the feedback a teacher provides. Figure 5.3 reports these findings.

Figure 5.3 illustrates that homework assigned but not commented on generates an effect size of only .28. When homework is graded, however, the effect size increases to .78. Finally, homework on which the teacher provides written comments for students has an effect size of .83, representing a percentile gain of 30 points.

Classroom Practice in Assigning Homework

1. Establish and communicate a homework policy. Students and their parents need to understand the purposes of homework, the amount of homework that will be assigned, consequences for not completing the homework, and a description of the types of parental involvement that are acceptable. Each of the generalizations in this chapter should be considered when establishing a policy that will be feasible and defensible. Whether districts, schools, or individual teachers establish these guidelines, communicating clearly with students and parents can decrease potential homework-related tensions that can grow between teachers and students, between parents and teachers, and between parents and their children. Establishing, communicating, and then adhering to clear policies also will increase the likelihood that homework will enhance student achievement. The following example illustrates what a homework policy might include and how teachers might communicate it to parents and students.

> One evening during the first week of school, Sharmine asked her parents to set aside 30 minutes to sit with her. Her teacher had given her a two-page homework policy, and they were to read it together. Further, both she and her parents had to sign it, and Sharmine had to return it the next day when all students would place the policy in front of

---

FIGURE 5.3

Research Results for Graded Homework

Use of Homework	No. of Effect Sizes (ESs)	Ave. ES	Percentile Gain
Homework with teachers' comments as feedback	2	.83	30
Graded homework	3	.78	28
Assigned homework but not graded or commented on	47	.28	11

their notebooks. Her parents were surprised when they saw the level of detail in the policy. Their older children had simply been told about the consequences for missing homework (usually points were deducted), but this policy explained much more. They were particularly pleased to see the following:

- ◆ Help set up a consistent organized place for homework to be done.
- ◆ Help your child establish either a consistent schedule for completing homework or help him create a schedule each Sunday night that reflects that particular week's activities.
- ◆ Encourage, motivate, and prompt your child, but do not sit with her and do the homework with her. The purpose of the homework is for your child to practice and use what she has learned. If your child is consistently not able to do the homework by herself, please contact the teacher.
- ◆ If your child is practicing a skill, ask him to tell you which steps are easy for him, which are difficult, or how he is going to improve. If your child is doing a project, ask him what knowledge he is applying in the project. If, your child is consistently unable to talk about the knowledge he is practicing or using, please call the teacher.
- ◆ Although there might be exceptions, the minutes your child should spend on homework should equal approximately 10 times her grade level (a 2nd grader would spend 20 minutes, a 3rd grader, 30, and so on).
- ◆ When bedtime comes, please stop your child, even if he is not done.

2. Design homework assignments that clearly articulate the purpose and outcome. The third generalization, discussed earlier in this chapter, explained that one purpose for homework is to provide time for students to practice what they have learned in class. A second is to prepare for new information or elaborate on information that has been introduced. Sometimes students do not distinguish between these two purposes. Some might even think that what their teachers really care about is that they simply complete the homework. Consequently, it is important to clearly identify the purpose of a given homework assignment and communicate that purpose. The following example describes how this might be done.

Carly opened her assignment notebook to record the homework for the evening. The pages for the assignment notebook had been copied for students at the beginning of the year so each page was organized the same, much like the templates provided in business daily calendars. For each day of the week, there were several squares organized as follows:

Subject: _____
Due Date: _____
What I have to do tonight: _____
Purpose of assignment: _____
What I have to already know or be able to do in order to complete the assignment: _____

At the beginning of the year, the teacher had reviewed how to fill out these squares. Although many students were a little overwhelmed when they first saw these pages, they soon became quite good at filling out each section quickly and concisely. One of the things they liked best about the "assignment squares" was that it gave them clear directions regarding what they were supposed to do and why they were being asked to do it.

3. Vary the approaches to providing feedback. Providing feedback on homework serves to enhance student achievement. Although the goal is to provide as much high-quality, specific feedback as possible, the reality is that not all homework will receive the same level of teacher attention. Many teachers try to grade and comment on each assignment, but when that is infeasible, they employ strategies that help them manage the workload and maximize the effectiveness of the feedback. The following example depicts one of these strategies.

If the homework for several nights in a row is on a single topic, the 5th grade students in Ms. Braun's class grade or discuss their own work in class the next morning and then place it in a portfolio kept in the classroom.

As frequently as possible, Ms. Braun reviews the work and makes specific comments on it. When Ms. Braun assigns homework to help students practice a skill to improve their speed and accuracy, she commonly explains to students that she would like them to provide some of their own feedback. Specifically, students are asked to keep track of their own speed and accuracy. If any students desire specific feedback from Ms. Braun, she schedules a time to discuss their progress with her.

Research and Theory Related to Practice

It is intuitively obvious that practice is necessary for learning knowledge of any type. In fact, the section on homework specifically mentioned the importance of practice. Here, we consider the specifics of practice in a little more depth. Figure 5.4 reports some of the results of studies that have attempted to synthesize the research on practice.

FIGURE 5.4
Research Results for Practice

Synthesis Study	Focus	No. of Effect Sizes (ESs)	Ave. ES	Percentile Gain
Ross, 1988	General effects of practice	9	1.29	40
Bloom, 1976[a]	General effects of practice	7 34 10	.54 .93 1.43	21 32 42
Kumar, 1991	General effects of practice	5	1.58	44

[a] Multiple effect sizes are listed for the Bloom study because of the manner in which effect sizes were reported. Readers should consult that study for more details.

FIGURE 5.5

Learning Line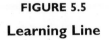

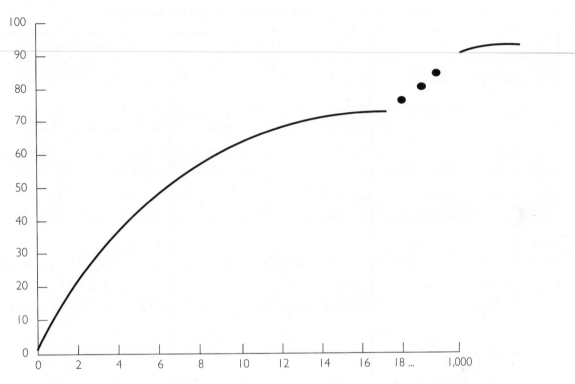

We have drawn two generalizations from the research on practice.

1. Mastering a skill requires a fair amount of focused practice. Research in cognitive psychology has demonstrated that skill learning commonly takes on a specific form (see Anderson, J. R., 1995; Newell & Rosenbloom, 1981). Figure 5.5 shows this form, the "learning line."

The vertical axis in Figure 5.5 represents improvement in learning. It is based on a 100-point scale, where a score of 100 represents complete mastery of the skill and a score of zero indicates no knowledge

of the skill. The horizontal axis represents the number of practice sessions in which a student has engaged. There are a few important things to note about Figure 5.5. First, notice how much practice it takes for students to reach a fair level of competence in a skill. It's not until students have practiced upwards of about 24 times that they reach 80-percent competency. Second, notice how the increase in competence is less and less after each practice. This is depicted rather dramatically in Figure 5.6.

Figure 5.6 indicates that the first four practice sessions result in a level of competence that is 47.9 percent of complete mas-

FIGURE 5.6

Increase in Learning Between Practice Sessions

Practice Session #	Increase in Learning (%)	Cumulative Increase (%)
1	22.918	22.918
2	11.741	34.659
3	7.659	42.318
4	5.593	47.911
5	4.349	52.26
6	3.534	55.798
7	2.960	58.754
8	2.535	61.289
9	2.205	63.494
10	1.945	65.439
11	1.740	67.179
12	1.562	68.741
13	1.426	70.167
14	1.305	71.472
15	1.198	72.670
16	1.108	73.778
17	1.034	74.812
18	.963	75.775
19	.897	76.672
20	.849	77.521
21	.802	78.323
22	.761	79.084
23	.721	79.805
24	.618	80.423

tery. The next four practice sessions, however, account for about a 14-percent increase only. Learning new content, then, does not happen quickly. It requires practice spread out over time. The results of such practice will be increments in learning that start out rather large but gradually get smaller and smaller as students fine tune their knowledge and skill. It is only after a great deal of practice that students can perform a skill with speed and accuracy.

2. While practicing, students should adapt and shape what they have learned. One finding from the research on practice that has strong classroom implications is that students must adapt or "shape" skills as they are learning them. In fact, one can think of skill learning as involving a "shaping phase." It is during this shaping phase that learners attend to their conceptual understanding of a skill. When students lack conceptual understanding of skills, they are liable to use procedures in shallow and ineffective ways (see Clement, Lockhead, & Mink, 1979; Davis, R. B., 1984; Mathematical Science Education Board, 1990; Romberg & Carpenter, 1986).

Apparently, it is important to deal with only a few examples during the shaping phase of learning a new skill or process. The shaping phase is not the time to press students to perform a skill with significant speed. Unfortunately, Healy (1990) reports that educators in the United States tend to prematurely engage students in a heavy practice schedule and rush them through multiple examples. In contrast, as Healy reports, Japanese educators attend to the needs of the shaping process by slowly walking through only a few examples:

> Whereas American second graders may spend thirty minutes on two or three pages of addition and subtraction equations, the Japanese are reported to be more likely at this level to use the same amount of time in examining two or three problems in depth, focusing on the reasoning process necessary to solve them (p. 281).

Classroom Practice Regarding Practicing Skills

Charting Accuracy and Speed

The first generalization regarding "practice" notes that skills should be learned to the level that students can perform them quickly and accurately. To facilitate skill development, students should be encouraged to keep track of their speed and accuracy. This might be best accomplished if they chart both. The following example shows how charting worked for one class in the context of analogy problems.

> Mrs. Cummings was helping her students expand their vocabulary, in part to prepare for the analogy section of the upcoming state test. She designed a series of homework assignments, in-class exercises, and tests that presented students with a wide variety of analogy problems. Students had 30 minutes to complete each test. For homework, students timed themselves as they took these tests, stopping at 30 minutes. At the end of each exercise or test, Mrs. Cummings reviewed the correct answers. Students kept track of the number of problems they completed in each 30-minute time period, as well as the number of problems they answered correctly. They then charted their speed and accuracy to see if their accuracy suffered as

their speed increased or if they were able to achieve increased accuracy *and* speed.

Designing Practice Assignments That Focus on Specific Elements of a Complex Skill or Process

The idea of "focused practice" is particularly important when students are practicing a complex, multistep skill or process, such as the research process, scientific inquiry, or the writing process. If, for example, there is some aspect of the process that is particularly troublesome for students, they might need to be given assignments that help them focus their practice on that one aspect. This type of practice is referred to as focused because the learner still engages in the overall skill or process, but targets one particular aspect to attend to. The following example shows how focused practice worked for one student in improving his writing skills.

Jackson had been writing essays and stories all year in his 8th grade language arts class but felt that he wasn't really getting that much better. Several of his friends felt the same. His teacher, always probing for feedback from his students, heard their frustration. In a class discussion, they decided to establish more of a focus when they were writing. Jackson suggested they work on writing better conclusions to paragraphs because so many of his conclusions were beginning to sound the same. For example, he began most of his final sentences with "In conclusion," or "As you can see." Even he was sick of this approach.

For the next two weeks, the teacher focused every writing assignment on constructing better conclusions. He sometimes used the students' own work and sometimes used sample paragraphs from which he removed the last sentence and then asked students to create a conclusion. As a result, Jackson began to see real progress in this one aspect of writing.

Planning Time for Students to Increase Their Conceptual Understanding of Skills or Processes

While planning curriculum, many teachers identify the skills and processes students must learn and then try to decide how much instructional and homework time will be dedicated to each skill or process. Teachers typically set time aside for modeling the skill or process, for providing guided practice with the steps of the skill or process, and then for assigning independent practice sessions. It is also important, however, that students *understand* how a skill or process works. It is during curriculum planning that a teacher must make a commitment to increasing students' understanding of skills and processes and then identifying activities to accomplish this instructional goal. The following example shows how planning for understanding might play out in a physical education class:

Maria, a second-year high school physical education teacher, could see that her students were anxious to get on the tennis courts and start practicing the serve that she had just demonstrated. "Hold on. You are not ready to practice. I want you to become a good server, but I also want you to understand what makes a good serve and to figure out what works best for you."

While the rest of the class worked on a skill she had taught earlier that semester, Maria worked with small groups of students on serving. She asked each student to perform their serve in slow motion and then had them "freeze" at various points in the serve. She then provided several variations of that particular part of the serve and explained the advantages and disadvantages of each. Students then tried the serve several times, again in slow motion, using the different variations. For homework, students were asked to describe which variations worked best for them and why they thought it worked.

◆ ◆ ◆

Homework and practice are ways of extending the school day and providing students with opportunities to refine and extend their knowledge. Teachers can use both of these practices as powerful instructional tools.

6

NONLINGUISTIC
REPRESENTATIONS

Mrs. Maly asked her 5th graders to put their heads down on their desks and close their eyes. She started reading aloud from the book, *A Street Through Time,* by Anne Millard. The book describes an old street that becomes inhabited by nomadic hunter-gatherers. Throughout the book, the period in which the story takes place keeps changing, as do the demands placed on the people living in the "street through time." As she read the first couple of pages, she described what she saw "in her mind." She asked her students to "see in their mind" what they were hearing her say. She also told students that they could interrupt her reading to ask questions (e.g., What does the roof on the hut look like? Did the people hurt when they got the plague?) When she finished reading the story, Mrs. Maly asked students to work independently drawing pictures of their "favorite scenes" from the images they had created in their minds.

The next day, students shared and explained their pictures in small groups. When they finished, each group drew a semantic web to depict the information from the story they thought was the most important. Mrs. Maly instructed students to use the first layer of the web to choose general terms that were common to all time periods described in the story (e.g., transportation, food, shelter, and work). The next layer of the web was devoted to examples and illustrations of the common terms during specific eras depicted in the book.

Mrs. Maly has made good use of a powerful aspect of learning—generating mental pictures to go along with information, as well as creating graphic representations for that information.

Research and Theory on Nonlinguistic Representations

Many psychologists adhere to what has been called the "dual-coding" theory of information storage (see Paivio, 1969, 1971, 1990). This theory postulates that knowledge is stored in two forms—a linguistic form and an imagery form. The linguistic mode is semantic in nature. As a metaphor, one might think of the linguistic mode as containing actual statements in long-term memory. The imagery mode, in contrast, is expressed as mental pictures or even physical sensations, such as smell, taste, touch, kinesthetic association, and sound (Richardson, 1983).

In this book, the imagery mode of representation is referred to as a *nonlinguistic representation*. The more we use both systems of representation—linguistic and non-linguistic—the better we are able to think about and recall knowledge. This is particularly relevant to the classroom, because studies have consistently shown that the primary way we present new knowledge to students is linguistic. We either talk to them about the new content or have them read about the new content (see Flanders, 1970). This means that students are commonly left to their own devices to generate nonlinguistic representations. When teachers help students in this kind of work, how-

ever, the effects on achievement are strong. It has even been shown that explicitly engaging students in the creation of nonlinguistic representations stimulates and increases activity in the brain (see Gerlic & Jausovec, 1999). Figure 6.1 summarizes findings from a variety of studies that have attempted to synthesize the research on nonlinguistic representation.

We have found two generalizations that can guide teachers in the use of nonlinguistic representations in the classroom.

1. A variety of activities produce nonlinguistic representations. Though we need to remember that the goal of instructional strategies in this section is to produce nonlinguistic representations of knowledge *in the minds of students*, it is also true that this can be accomplished in many ways. Research indicates that each of the following activities enhances the development of nonlinguistic representations in students and, therefore, enhances their understanding of that content:

• *Creating graphic representations* (Alvermann & Boothby, 1986; Armbruster, Anderson, & Meyer, 1992; Darch, Carnine, & Kameenui, 1986; Griffin, Simmons, & Kameenui, 1992; Horton, Lovitt, & Bergerud, 1990; McLaughlin, 1991; Robinson & Kiewra, 1996).
• *Making physical models* (Welch, 1997).

FIGURE 6.1

Research Results for Nonlinguistic Representation

Synthesis Study	Focus	No. of Effect Sizes (ESs)	Ave. ES	Percentile Gain
Mayer, 1989[a]	General Nonlinguistic Techniques	10 16	1.02 1.31	34 40
Athappilly, Smidchens, & Kofel, 1980	General Nonlinguistic Techniques	39	.510	19
Powell, 1980 [a]	General Nonlinguistic Techniques	13 6 4	1.01 1.16 .56	34 38 21
Hattie et al., 1996	General Nonlinguistic Techniques	9	.91	32
Walberg, 1999 [a]	General Nonlinguistic Techniques	24 64	.56 1.04	21 35
Guzzetti, Snyder, & Glass, 1993	General Nonlinguistic Techniques	3	.51	20
Fletcher, 1990	General Nonlinguistic Techniques	47	.50	20

[a] Multiple effect sizes are listed because of the manner in which the effect sizes were reported. Readers should consult those studies for more details.

• *Generating mental pictures* (Muehlherr & Siermann, 1996; Willoughby, Desmarias, Wood, Sims, & Kalra, 1997).

• *Drawing pictures and pictographs* (Macklin, 1997; Newton, 1995; Pruitt, 1993).

• *Engaging in kinesthetic activity* (Aubusson, Foswill, Barr, & Perkovic, 1997; Druyan, 1997).

2. Nonlinguistic representations should elaborate on knowledge. In simple terms, elaboration involves "adding to" knowledge. For example, a student elaborates on his knowledge of fractions when

he constructs a mental model of how a fraction might appear in concrete form. When students elaborate on knowledge, they not only understand it in greater depth, but they can recall it much more easily (Pressley, Symons, McDaniel, Snyder, & Turnure, 1988; Woloshyn, Willoughby, Wood, & Pressley, 1990). Fortunately, the process of generating nonlinguistic representations engages students in elaborative thinking (see Anderson, J. R., 1990). That is, when a student generates a nonlinguistic representation of knowledge, by definition, she has elaborated on it. Finally, the power of elaboration can be enhanced by asking students to explain and justify their elaborations (Willoughby et al., 1997).

Classroom Practice in Nonlinguistic Representation

Creating Graphic Organizers

Graphic organizers are perhaps the most common way to help students generate nonlinguistic representations. One of the most comprehensive treatments of the use of graphic organizers can be found in the book *Visual Tools for Constructing Knowledge* by David Hyerle (1996). Actu-

ally, graphic organizers combine the *linguistic mode* in that they use words and phrases, and the *nonlinguistic mode* in that they use symbols and arrows to represent relationships. The following six graphic organizers have great utility in the classroom because they correspond to six common patterns into which most information can be organized: descriptive patterns, time-sequence patterns, process/cause-effect patterns, episode patterns, generalization/principle patterns, and concept patterns.

Descriptive Patterns. Descriptive patterns can be used to represent facts about specific persons, places, things, and events. The information organized into a descriptive pattern does not need to be in any particular order. Figure 6.2 shows how teach-

FIGURE 6.2

Descriptive Pattern Organizer

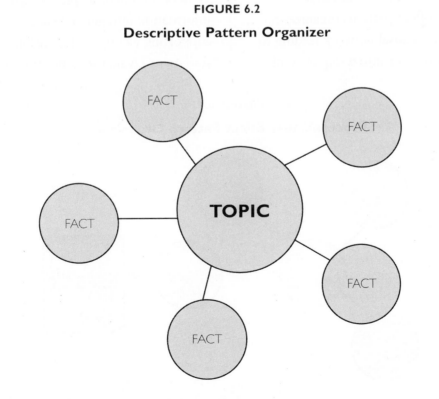

FIGURE 6.3

Time Sequence Pattern Organizer

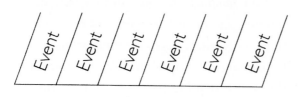

ers and students can graphically represent a descriptive pattern.

Time-Sequence Patterns. Time-sequence patterns organize events in a specific chronological order. For example, information about the development of the Apollo space program can be organized as a sequence pattern. Figure 6.3 shows how you might represent a time-sequence pattern graphically.

Process/Cause-Effect Patterns. Process/cause-effect patterns organize information into a causal network leading to a specific outcome or into a sequence of steps leading to a specific product. For example, information about the factors that typically lead to the development of a healthy body might be organized as a process/cause-effect pattern. Figure 6.4 shows a graphic representation of a process/cause-effect pattern.

Episode Patterns. Episode patterns organize information about specific events, including (1) a setting (time and place), (2) specific people, (3) a specific duration, (4) a specific sequence of events, and (5) a particular cause and effect. For example, students might organize information about the French Revolution into an episode pattern using a graphic like that shown in Figure 6.5.

Generalization/Principle Patterns. Generalization/principle patterns organize information into general statements with supporting examples. For instance, for the statement, "A mathematics function is a re-

FIGURE 6.4

Process/Cause-Effect Pattern Organizer

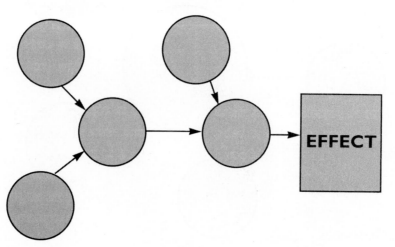

FIGURE 6.5

Episode Pattern Organizer

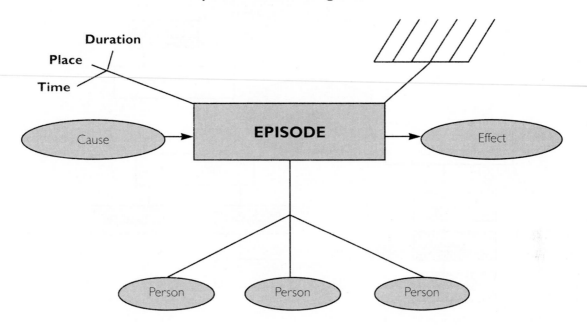

lationship where the value of one variable depends on the value of another variable," students can provide and represent examples in a graphic like that shown in Figure 6.6.

Concept Patterns. Concept patterns, the most general of all patterns, organize information around a word or phrase that represents entire classes or categories of persons, places, things, and events. The characteristics or attributes of the concept, along with examples of each, should be included in this pattern. For example, students could use a graphic like the one in Figure 6.7 to organize the concept of *fables*, along with examples and characteristics.

The following example shows how a student might use more than one graphic organizer with a single topic.

When Ty Crocker studied for his test on Law and the Legal System, he found a good way to remember the three common methods for solving disputes out of court. He matched each of the three methods, *ar-*

FIGURE 6.6

Generalization/Principle Pattern Organizer

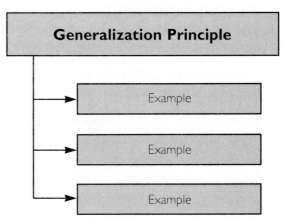

FIGURE 6.7

Concept Pattern Organizer

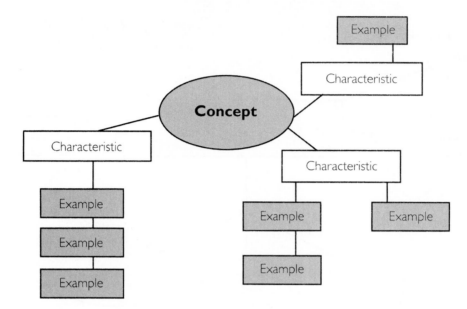

bitration, *negotiation*, and *voluntary mediation*, to a different kind of graphic organizer he had learned in his English class. For the topic of *arbitration*, he used a "time-sequence pattern." For *negotiation*, he used a "process or cause-effect pattern." He created a "concept pattern" for *voluntary mediation*. Figures 6.8–6.10 (pp. 79–80) show these graphic representations.

Using Other Nonlinguistic Representations

Making Physical Models. As the name implies, physical models are concrete representations of the knowledge that is being learned. Mathematics and science teachers commonly refer to the use of concrete representations as "manipulatives." The very

act of generating a concrete representation establishes an "image" of the knowledge in students' minds. The following example illustrates this process in the context of a science class.

Mrs. Allison helped her 4th grade class to understand why we see different phases of the moon by presenting a concrete representation of the moon's monthly journey around the earth and its relationship to the sun. For the moon, Mrs. Allison gave each student a white Styrofoam ball and had them stick it on the end of a pencil. For the sun, she used a lamp with the shade removed. She told her students each of them would be the earth.

Mrs. Allison placed the lamp in the middle of the room, pulled down the window shades, and turned off the lights. Then she had each student place the ball at arm's

FIGURE 6.8

Time-Sequence Pattern in Arbitration

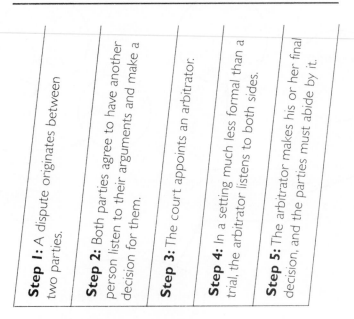

Step 1: A dispute originates between two parties.

Step 2: Both parties agree to have another person listen to their arguments and make a decision for them.

Step 3: The court appoints an arbitrator.

Step 4: In a setting much less formal than a trial, the arbitrator listens to both sides.

Step 5: The arbitrator makes his or her final decision, and the parties must abide by it.

FIGURE 6.9

Process/Cause-Effect Pattern for Negotiation

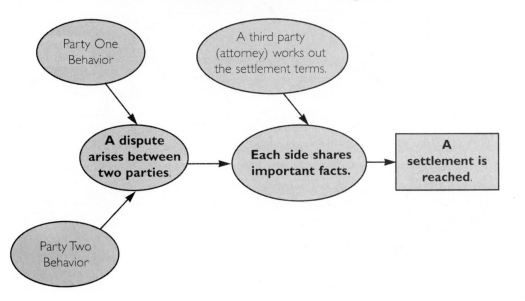

Party One Behavior

A third party (attorney) works out the settlement terms.

A dispute arises between two parties.

Each side shares important facts.

A settlement is reached.

Party Two Behavior

FIGURE 6.10

Concept Pattern for Voluntary Mediation

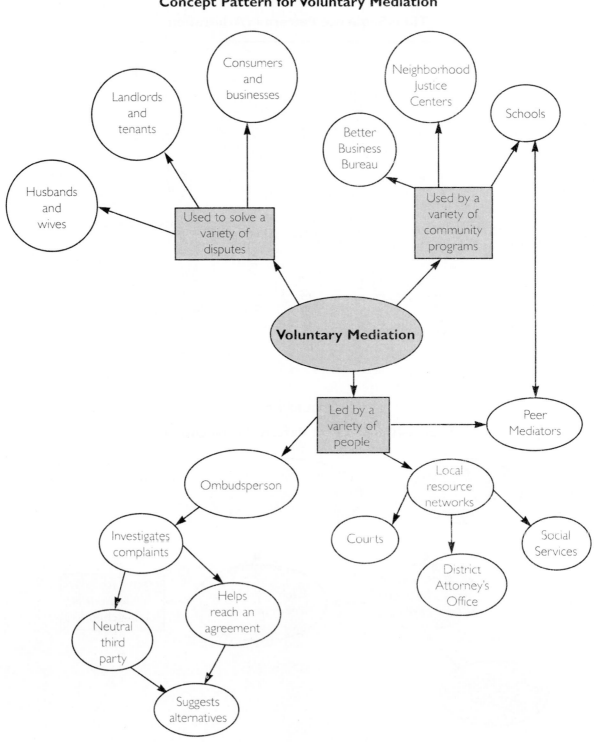

length between the bulb and their eyes, simulating a total solar eclipse, which, she explained, is quite rare. Because the moon usually passes above or below the sun as viewed from Earth, Mrs. Allison then had her students move their moon up or down a bit so that they were looking into the Sun. From this position the students could observe that all the sunlight was shining on the far side of the moon, opposite the side they were viewing, simulating a new moon.

Mrs. Allison guided her students to move their moons in such a way that they observed first a crescent moon, then a half moon, a full moon, and a three-quarter moon. At each point, Mrs. Allison pointed out that the sun was always illuminating half of the moon (except in the case of a lunar eclipse) and that the appearance of the these fractions of moon was due to the moon's changing position in relationship to the earth over the course of a month.

Generating Mental Pictures. The most direct way to generate nonlinguistic representations is to simply construct (i.e., imagine) a mental picture of knowledge being learned. For abstract content, these mental pictures might be highly symbolic. To illustrate, psychologist John Hayes (1981) provides an example of how a student might generate a mental picture for the following equation from physics:

$$F = \frac{(M_1 M_2)G}{r^2}$$

The equation states that force (F) is equal to the product of the masses of two objects (M_1 and M_2) times a constant (G) divided by the square of the distance between them r^2. There are a number of ways this information might be represented symbolically. Hayes suggests an image of two large globes in space with the learner in the middle trying to hold them apart:

If either of the globes were very heavy, we would expect that it would be harder to hold them apart than if both were light. Since force increases as either of the masses (M_1 and M_2) increases, the masses must be in the numerator. As we push the globes further apart, the force of attraction between them will decrease as the force of attraction between two magnets decreases as we pull them apart. Since force decreases as distance increases, r must be in the denominator (p. 126).

The following example shows how a teacher might facilitate the construction of mental pictures in the context of a social studies class.

Mr. Williams's 5th grade class is beginning a unit on the history of Native American cultures in the southwest United States. To begin, Mr. Williams introduces his students to the strategy of creating mental pictures of information and ideas. He tells them to imagine that they are early European explorers who have stumbled on the abandoned cliff palace of Mesa Verde. He has them close their eyes and imagine they are traveling by horseback through the canyon lands. He has them "feel" the hot desert sunlight, "see" the scrubby vegetation, and "smell" the junipers and piñon pines.

"Imagine," Mr. Williams says, "that you suddenly see something in the distance that looks like an apartment building carved into a cliff. Would you be puzzled? Curious? Frightened? Now imagine that you gallop your horse to the edge of the cliff and peer across at the black and tan sandstone and yes, it is something like an apartment building. There are ladders, black hole windows, and circular pits, but no people. It's absolutely quiet. There's no sign of life. Would you wonder what happened to the people who lived there? What would you think about the builders of this mysterious structure? Would you be brave enough to go inside? What do you think you would find?"

Drawing Pictures and Pictographs.
Drawing pictures or pictographs (i.e., symbolic pictures) to represent knowledge is a powerful way to generate nonlinguistic representations in the mind. For example, most students have either drawn or colored the human skeletal system or have seen a picture of one in the classroom. Similarly, most students have drawn or colored a representation of the solar system. A variation of a picture is the pictograph, which is a drawing that uses symbols or symbolic pictures to represent information. The following example shows how a 1st grade teacher uses symbolic pictures in a geography lesson.

Allison Mason's 1st graders always have a hard time understanding the abstract idea that the northern hemisphere tilts toward and away from the sun, causing summer and winter. She asks the students to draw a picture of the earth's movement as she de-

scribes each season. Zach draws the picture shown in Figure 6.11. Based on the picture, Ms. Mason and Zach have a conversation about the earth's tilt. When Zach draws in the equator, he finally begins to understand what she means about the earth "tilting."

Engaging in Kinesthetic Activity.
Kinesthetic activities are those that involve physical movement. By definition, physical movement associated with specific knowledge generates a mental image of the knowledge in the mind of the learner. (Recall from the previous discussion that mental images include physical sensations.) Most children find this both a natural and enjoyable way to express their knowledge. The following example below illustrates this in the context of a math class.

Often, to take a brief pause in math class, Ms. Jenkins asks her 4th grade students to think of ways they can represent what they are learning. For example, during the lesson on radius, diameter, and circumference of circles, Barry uses his left arm outstretched to show radius, both arms outstretched to show diameter, and both arms forming a circle to show circumference. During a different lesson on angles, Devon depicts obtuse and acute angles by making wide and not-so-wide "Vs" with her arms as the children yell out the degrees. They even have ways to show fractions, mixed numbers, and turning fractions into their simplest forms.

Ms. Jenkins started the activity she called *Body Math* just to give the students a break

FIGURE 6.11

Student Pictograph

from the routine of doing math drills, but then realized that it was a powerful way for students to show whether or not they understood the concept behind the problems. Once the word got around, other students could be seen peeking in the classroom to see what they were doing that day with body math.

♦ ♦ ♦

Probably the most underused instructional strategy of all those reviewed in this book—creating nonlinguistic representations—helps students understand content in a whole new way. As we have seen, teachers can take a variety of approaches, ranging from graphic organizers to physical models.

7

Cooperative
Learning

Ms. Cimino's middle school class was beginning a unit on the regions of the United States. One of her goals was for students to understand how diverse the regions are. Ms. Cimino explained to students that they would be working in small groups to create a class presentation about a particular region. Each presentation, which would be made in class in two weeks, was to cover the geography, weather patterns, and economic/cultural activities of the region. Ms. Cimino told students that they could use the resources in the classroom, the library, or any of three Internet sites she had identified.

To facilitate the groupwork, Ms. Cimino began by dividing the class into groups of three and assigning a region to each group. Within each group, students agreed who would be the overall leader or organizer, the recorder of the group's discussions, and so on. Each group also decided how they would divide up the work; because there were three students in each group, most groups divided the research into the three areas of focus Ms. Cimino had specified for the presentations. Ms. Cimino encouraged each group to take time every couple of days to evaluate each individual's progress, as well as the group's overall progress; to solve any problems they were encountering; and to fine-tune their work as needed. Ms. Cimino met with each group periodically to monitor their progress, help them solve problems, and help them work together more effectively.

Ms. Cimino used one of the most popular instructional strategies in education—cooperative learning.

Research and Theory on Cooperative Learning

The specific topic of this chapter is cooperative learning. One might view this topic, however, as falling within the more general one of "grouping" strategies. The practice of grouping can be traced back to at least 1867 when educational reformer W. T. Harris initiated a plan in St. Louis, Missouri, that allowed for the rapid promotion of students through the elementary grades. According to Kulik and Kulik (1982), the Harris plan "represented a first step toward ability grouped classrooms" (p. 415). It wasn't until the turn of the century, however, that a version of grouping was implemented that mirrored current practice. Specifically, in the Santa Barbara Plan, each grade was divided into A, B, and C sections. Although each grade mastered the same basic content, the A group addressed the content in more depth than the B group, who addressed the content in more depth than the C group.

In 1982, Kulik and Kulik noted: "Today, thousands of American schools follow this model of homogeneous grouping" (p. 416). It is probably safe to say that since Kulik and Kulik's observations in 1982, the practice of forming whole classes on the basis of ability has decreased dramatically. One reason for this might be the relatively small effect size associated with this practice. For example, in their analysis of 52 studies carried out in secondary schools, Kulik and Kulik found an average effect size of only .10 for ability grouping by class. Another reason for the decline in this practice might be that many educators have made strong claims that ability grouping promotes inequity—in other words, it does little to narrow the gap between the "low ability students and the middle and high ability students" (see Oakes, 1985). Given that in this book we focus only on those instructional variables over which a teacher has control, we are not including in this chapter a discussion of the various ways a school might organize students into homogeneous classes. Rather, the focus of this chapter is the ways a teacher might organize her students within a heterogeneous class.

From the title of this chapter, it is obvious that we recommend the use of "cooperative" grouping strategies. According to David Johnson and Roger Johnson (1999), recognized leaders in the field of cooperative learning, there are five defining elements of cooperative learning:

◆ *Positive interdependence* (a sense of sink or swim together).
◆ *Face-to-face promotive interaction* (helping each other learn, applauding success and efforts).
◆ *Individual and group accountability* (each of us has to contribute to the group achieving its goals).

◆ *Interpersonal and small group skills* (communication, trust, leadership, decision making, and conflict resolution).

◆ *Group processing* (reflecting on how well the team is functioning and how to function even better) [Compiled from the Web site (http://www.clcrc.com/index. html#essays) of the Cooperative Learning Center at the University of Minnesota, codirected by Johnson and Johnson].

Figure 7.1 summarizes results from some of the studies that have attempted to synthesize the research in cooperative learning.

Of the studies listed in Figure 7.1, the one most commonly cited is the 1981 study by Johnson and others. Perhaps most noteworthy about this research synthesis is that it contrasted cooperative learning with several related techniques, three of which are reported in Figure 7.1: intergroup competition, individual competition, and use of individual student tasks. Johnson and colleagues found that cooperative learning groups and groups that engage in intergroup competition produce the same effect on student learning; this is indicated by the .00 effect size when the two are compared—there were no differences in achievement between the experimental and control groups. But cooperative learning has an effect size of .78 when compared with strategies in which students compete with each other (individual com-

FIGURE 7.1

Research Results for Cooperative Learning

Synthesis Study	Focus	No. of Effect Sizes (ESs)	Ave. ES	Percentile Gain
Walberg, 1999	Cooperative learning (general)	182	.78	28
Lipsey & Wilson, 1993	Cooperative learning (general)	414	.63	23
Scheerens & Bosker, 1997	Cooperative learning (general)	—	.50	21
Hall, 1989	Cooperative learning (general)	37	.30	12
Johnson, D., Maruyama, Johnson, R., Nelson, & Skon, 1981	Cooperative learning (general)	122	.73	27
	Cooperative vs. intergroup competition	9	.00	0
	Cooperative vs. individual competition	70	.78	28
	Cooperative vs. individual student tasks	104	.78	28

FIGURE 7.2

Homogenous Grouping Versus No Grouping

Synthesis Study	Focus	No. of Effect Sizes (ESs)	Ave. ES	Percentile Gain
Slavin, 1987	Ability grouping (general)	7	.32	12
Kulik & Kulik, 1987	Ability grouping (general)	15	.17	6
Kulik & Kulik, 1991	Ability grouping (general)	11	.25	10
Lou et al., 1996	Ability grouping (general)	103	.17	6
	Low-ability students	24	.37	14
	Medium-ability students	11	.19	7
	High-ability students	18	.28	11

petition). Finally, cooperative learning has an effect size of .78 when compared with instructional strategies in which students work on tasks individually without competing with one another (individual student tasks). In general, then, organizing students in cooperative learning groups has a powerful effect on learning, regardless of whether groups compete with one another.

Three generalizations can be used to guide the use of cooperative learning:

1. Organizing groups based on ability levels should be done sparingly. One of the more controversial aspects of organizing students in groups (whether they be cooperative groups or otherwise) is whether the groups should be homogeneous—organized by ability levels. In general, homogenous grouping seems to have a positive effect on student achievement when compared with no grouping. Figure 7.2 reports results from some of the synthesis studies.

Of great importance to this discussion are the Lou and others (1996) findings that students of all ability levels benefit from ability grouping when compared with no grouping at all. Equally important, however, are the findings reported in Figure 7.3, which shows the results from studies that compared homogeneous versus heterogeneous grouping.

As shown in Figure 7.3, students of low ability actually perform worse when they are placed in homogeneous groups with students of low ability—as opposed to students of low ability placed in heterogeneous groups. This is evidenced by the negative effect size of −.60. In addition, the effect of homogeneous grouping on high-ability students is positive but small (.09). It is the medium-ability students who benefit the most from homogeneous grouping (ES = .51). Grouping students by ability, then, might have very different effects on different students—the experience of stu-

FIGURE 7.3

Homogeneous Versus Heterogeneous Grouping

Ability Level of Students	No. of Effect Sizes (ESs)	Ave. ES	Percentile Gain[a]
Low ability	4	−.60	−23
Medium ability	4	.51	19
High ability	5	.09	3

[a] Data from Lou et al., 1996.

dents in the low-ability group might be quite different from that of the experience of students in the middle- and high-ability groups (Webb, 1982).

2. Cooperative groups should be kept rather small in size. This generalization might appear obvious, but it is certainly worth mentioning. Specifically, Lou and others (1996) reported the effect sizes shown in Figure 7.4.

These findings led Lou and colleagues to recommend: "Small teams of three to four members seem more effective than larger groups" (1996, p. 451).

3. Cooperative learning should be applied consistently and systematically, but not overused. Cooperative learning is an instructional strategy that works best when applied systematically. In fact, Lou and colleagues (1996) report that grouping strategies are most effective when applied at least once a week. Some psychologists, however, warn against the "overuse" of cooperative learning. Specifically, researchers John Anderson, Lynne Reder, and Herbert Simon (1997) warn that cooperative learning can be misused and is frequently overused in education: it is *misused* when the tasks given to cooperative groups are not well structured; it is *overused* when it is implemented to such an extent that students have an insufficient amount of time

FIGURE 7.4

Size of Groups

Group Size	No. of Effect Sizes (ESs)	Ave. ES	Percentile Gain
Pairs	13	.15	6
3–4	38	.22	9
5–7	17	−.02	−1

to practice independently the skills and processes that they must master.

Classroom Practice in Cooperative Learning

Using a Variety of Criteria for Grouping Students

When considering how to group students, remember that Generalization 1 suggests that *ability* grouping should be used sparingly. Indeed, students can be grouped according to interest, according to their birthday month, according to the colors they are wearing, alphabetically, or even randomly by picking names from a hat. To maximize students' experience, it is probably a good idea to use a variety of criteria, as well as to adhere to the tenets of cooperative learning, to make the experience successful. Kagan (1994) suggests a variety of group structures. The following example describes the perspective of a student who experienced different types of cooperative learning groups.

Tommy had not been happy when he heard that in 4th grade science the students would be working in groups all year. Most of his experience with groups was in math, where he was always in what he called "the math for dummies" group. He hated it. But, as he listened to the science teacher, he began to understand how these groups would be formed and how often they would change. First, the teacher explained that they would be in

groups about half of the time only. Then she explained that for the first unit, they would be placed in groups based on the type of pets they had. This would give them some common experiences on which to build discussions of animals and their habits. If too many students had the same pets, such as a dog and a cat, or if only one student had a pet, for example, an iguana, they would mix and match until the groups were small but shared some common experiences with animals. Tommy decided groups might be okay, after all.

Informal, Formal, and Base Groups

One way to vary the grouping patterns within a class is to use the three types of cooperative learning groups identified by Johnson and Johnson (1999)—informal, formal, and base groups. Informal groups (e.g., pair-share, turn-to-your-neighbor) are ad hoc groups that last from a few minutes to a class period. They can be used to clarify expectations for tasks, focus students' attention, allow students time to more deeply process information, or to provide time for closure. The following example depicts how a teacher might use informal groups of two while reading to students.

Mr. Anderson likes to read aloud original source documents about slavery to his 5th graders. After reading for 10 minutes, he gives the students a discussion task to complete in pairs for 3–4 minutes. The task requires students to answer a specific question that he provides. After each member of a pair formulates a response and discusses it with his partner, Mr. Anderson begins to read aloud again. After 10 minutes, Mr. Anderson stops and asks students to complete a second paired discussion task. Occasionally, he asks two or three pairs to share a brief summary of their discussions. At the end of the class, Mr. Anderson asks the paired students to summarize what they have learned from the readings and discussions in written form and turn their summaries in to him.

Formal groups are designed to ensure that the students have enough time to thoroughly complete an academic assignment; therefore, they may last for several days or even weeks. When using formal groups, the teacher designs tasks to include the basic cooperative learning components:

- ◆ Positive interdependence.
- ◆ Group processing.
- ◆ Appropriate use of social skills.
- ◆ Face-to-face promotive interaction.
- ◆ Individual and group accountability

(Johnson & Johnson, 1999).

The following example shows the use of formal groups in the context of a complex task.

Ms. Randall begins her high school economics lesson on trade and consumers by asking her 32 students to form eight groups of 4 by counting off from 1 to 8. The group members are each assigned a role: recorder, summarizer, technical advisor, and researcher. Each group is given the task of creating a product, using specific guidelines she has provided them. Over the course of four days, the students will work together to decide on a product, design it, and create a marketing display. They will try to sell their products to the other teams. Ms. Randall sys-

tematically monitors individuals and groups for social skills, problem-solving strategies, and group processing. She often asks students to self-assess on specific skills. In the final presentation of the product, students must demonstrate their individual contributions, as well as the accomplishments of the group as a whole.

Base groups are long-term groups (e.g., for the semester or year) created to provide students with support throughout a semester or an academic year. The following example shows the use of base groups in a 3rd grade class.

When Mrs. Ramos told Mr. Stalls that it was the fourth week of school and she noticed that her 3rd graders still didn't know each other by name, he suggested that she create base groups. She had heard of using base groups before to accomplish routine tasks and provide support for students, but thought they were useful for older students only.

After she organized students into base groups, she asked them to take a few minutes to exchange phone numbers and share any schedule information that they should know about each other (e.g., soccer practices, piano lessons, and scouting). She explained that each day they would meet in their base groups for five minutes to greet each other, check to make sure homework was turned in, and sign up for lunch choices. At the end of the day, they would also meet to review homework assignments and help each other with classroom chores.

Over the course of the year, the students stayed in these base groups. In addition to completing routine tasks, the base groups planned activities, ran errands (e.g., collecting all of the class library books and taking them to the media center on a cart), and had fun (e.g., teams on the field day). As a result of the base groups, Mrs. Ramos noticed a difference in the students' general sense of belonging to the class.

Managing Group Size

As described in Generalization 2, cooperative groups should be kept small. Although a given task may appear suited to a large group, students may not have the skills to work competently in a large group. Many teachers suggest that the rule of thumb is "the smaller the better." However, sometimes resources may dictate the use of bigger groups. One of the management tasks for a teacher is to continually monitor the size of the groups he is using, making changes when warranted.

Mr. Eden's students were in the media center working on their Constitution projects. Steve asked if he could talk for a few minutes about their group because it wasn't working very well. "There is definitely enough to do and we understand the assignment, but there are just too many of us," he said. Mr. Eden watched the group for a while and realized that Steve was right. That afternoon, Mr. Eden reorganized the students into triads, instead of groups of six. It took some extra time to rearrange the tasks and reassign the work, but in the long run, he realized that he had complicated the task for students by using groups that were too large.

Combining Cooperative Learning with Other Classroom Structures

Even teachers who are extremely committed to using cooperative learning groups would agree with Generalization 3, that cooperative learning can be overused. Any strategy, in fact, can be overused and lose its effectiveness. The following example describes the experience of a teacher who had to be reminded of this.

Ms. Mandrell was a cooperative learning zealot and a master at using it in her 8th grade class. She, therefore, could not figure out why lately it seemed the groups in her class were not getting along and were not as productive as she had observed earlier in the year. She had even tried allowing students to select their own groups, a practice she rarely used, but this did not seem to help.

Finally, during group processing, she shared her observations with the students. One student helped identify the problem, "We need some alone time. I'm tired of interacting all the time. I need to have more time to just think and work quietly."

Other students chimed in, "We like to work with each other, but not so much. I learn some things better on my own."

Ms. Mandrell heard the message. "You're right. I get obsessive when I like something and I like cooperative learning. But keep reminding me if I get carried away again. I promise I'll listen."

◆ ◆ ◆

Of all classroom grouping strategies, cooperative learning may be the most flexible and powerful. As the examples in this chapter illustrate, teachers can use cooperative learning in a variety of ways in many different situations.

8

SETTING OBJECTIVES AND PROVIDING FEEDBACK

Every year Mr. Hall gave the same motivational speech to the students in his Advanced Placement United States History course reminding them that although they were the ones taking the AP test, their scores reflected his teaching. In the past, classes had performed reasonably well, but he always felt a pang of guilt; he wanted to do more to help students pass the test with 4s and 5s. However, his previous attempts had not produced the results he wanted.

One summer, he outlined all the units in the chapters in great detail, color-coded them, and gave the outline to his students as study guides. The students found them useful, but became dependent on the guides. They also admitted that they ignored any information that he had not included in his outlines.

Another year, he focused on improving their study skills by offering Saturday classes on how to take tests, but students didn't seem to do better on the AP test. This year, instead of constructing a detailed outline, Mr. Hall wrote generalizations for each era they would study in class. He used the generalizations that were provided in the national standards and benchmarks. For each era, he also provided a set of key vocabulary terms, highlighting the ones that would recur throughout various units.

He explained to students that they should create a study journal for themselves in which they identified their own learning goals based on the generalizations he provided. He modeled the process for the first unit, showing them how to use the generalizations as a springboard for identifying the specific things they wanted to learn. He referred to this whole process as "goal setting for learning." Most of the students were a bit confused at first because in the past they had set goals focused on "tasks," not on their "understandings." The unit on the Civil War included generalizations on what led to the conflict.

One student, Paul, wrote the generalization at the top of the page. Then he wrote a personal learning goal that read, "I plan to learn if there is more than one theory about the causes of the U.S. Civil War. I always heard that it was started because of slavery. I'd like to know more about the beginnings of the war." In his study journal, Paul wrote the phrase "causes of the Civil War" and put a big circle around it. He then drew four lines with arrows connecting it to different phrases: (1) north/south conflicting views of slavery, (2) westward expansion, (3) the theory that history happens, and (4) "because of industrialization." During the week he added facts and cleared up misconceptions in each of the four areas he had identified, and by the end of the week (using information from readings and lectures) he had summarized the causes of the Civil War. Other students organized their ideas differently.

Mr. Hall encouraged students to share their personal learning goals and what they learned as the unit progressed. At least once a week, Mr. Hall would meet individually with all the students to see how they were progressing with their goals, even if it was just for a couple of minutes. Because he gave quizzes and tests along the way, he was able to check each student's progress by drawing a relationship between their grades and the goals they had set for their learning.

Mr. Hall used goal setting and feedback in a precise and sophisticated manner to enhance his students' learning. Both of these activities engage what many researchers and theorists refer to as the *metacognitive* system of thinking.

Research and Theory on Goal Setting

Broadly defined, goal setting is the process of establishing a direction for learning. It is a skill that successful people have mastered to help them realize both short-term and long-term desires. Figure 8.1 reports findings from some of the studies that have at-

---

FIGURE 8.1

Research Results for Goal Setting

Synthesis Study	Focus	No. of Effect Sizes (ESs)	Ave. ES	Percentile Gain
Wise & Okey, 1983[a]	General effects of setting goals or objectives	3 25	1.37 .48	41 18
Walberg, 1999	General effects of setting goals or objectives	21	.46	18
Lipsey & Wilson, 1993	General effects of setting goals or objectives	204	.55	21

[a] Two effect sizes are listed because of the manner in which effect sizes were reported. Readers should consult that study for more details.

tempted to synthesize the research on goal setting.

We have drawn three generalizations from the research on goal setting:

1. Instructional goals narrow what students focus on. One of the more interesting findings in the research is the negative effect that setting goals or objectives has on outcomes other than those specified in the objectives. Specifically, in his analysis of 20 studies involving instructional goals, Walberg (1999) reported that they have an effect size of $-.20$ on "unintended outcomes." This means that if a teacher establishes a goal, for example, that students understand how a cell functions, students' understanding of information incidental to this concept, but still addressed in class, might actually be less than if a specific goal were not set. In fact, an effect size of $-.20$ indicates that the average student in the class where specific goals about the cell were set, would score 8 percentile points lower than a student in a class where these goals were not set, *in a test of information that did not pertain to the cell.* At first, this might seem counter intuitive, but with a little reflection, these findings actually make a great deal of sense. This phenomenon might occur because setting a goal focuses students' attention to such a degree that they ignore information not specifically related to the goal.

2. Instructional goals should not be too specific. One fairly stable finding in the literature on goal setting is that instructional goals stated in behavioral objective format do not produce effect sizes as high as instructional goals stated in more general formats. Specifically, in their analysis of 111 studies on behavioral objectives, Fraser and others (1987) found the average effect size to be .12, which translates into a gain of only 5 percentile points. A plausible explanation is that behavioral objectives are simply too specific.

Behavioral objectives gained prominence in 1962 when evaluation expert Robert Mager published the book *Preparing Instructional Objectives.* He explained that effective instructional objectives contain three defining characteristics:

> 1. *Performance.* An objective always says what a learner is expected to be able to do; the objective sometimes describes the product or result of the doing.
> 2. *Conditions.* An objective always describes the important conditions (if any) under which the performance is to occur.
> 3. *Criterion.* Whenever possible, an objective describes the criterion of acceptable performance by describing how well the learner must perform in order to be considered acceptable (p. 21).

Instructional objectives generated using Mager's criteria are obviously highly specific in nature. Perhaps they are simply too specific to accommodate the individual and constructivist nature of the learning process.

3. Students should be encouraged to personalize the teacher's goals. Once the teacher has established classroom learning goals, students should be encouraged to adapt them to their personal needs and desires. This is one of the reasons goals should not be too specific. That is, if goals are stated in highly specific, behavioral objective format, they are not amenable to being adapted by students. Some studies have demonstrated the positive effects of students' setting goals in a "contractual" context. That is, students not only identify the goals they will try to attain (within the framework of the larger goals established by the teacher), but they also contract for the grade they will receive if they meet those goals (see Kahle & Kelly, 1994; Miller & Kelley, 1994; Vollmer, 1995). Other studies have demonstrated the positive effects of students' setting "subgoals" (Bandura & Schunk, 1981; Morgan, 1985).

Classroom Practice in Goal Setting

Specific but Flexible Goals

It is certainly important for a teacher to set goals for students, but it is also important for the goals to be general enough to provide students with some flexibility. The following example shows how this might occur in a health unit.

The students in Ms. Gershwin's 4th grade class have been setting their own personal goals for each unit since the beginning of the year. She always provides the general targets, but then students personalize the goals. For the unit on the Human Body, she explains that her goal is for them to understand how each of the main organs works individually, as well as how the organs work together as a system. Based on those broad goals, Josh writes his personal learning goals.

I want to know more about the kidneys and how they work. My grandpa is having a kidney replaced soon.
I know that the heart pumps blood through the body, but *I want to know* how a heart attack happens.
I want to know if the intestines are really four miles long.

Ms. Gershwin found that if she provided the sentence stems (e.g., "I want to know..." and "I want to know more ..."), the students were able to create more interesting specific goals.

Contracts

One variation on goal setting is to contract with students for the attainment of specific goals. This provides students with a great deal of control over their learning. The following example shows how a middle school teacher used contracts in the context of a technology class.

Mrs. Rome was excited about teaching the three-week unit on "Making Your Own Web Site" to the middle-school students, but wary because the students would clearly vary in their experiences with computers. To respond to these differences, she prepared a packet that students could work through at their own pace. The packet identified what the students needed to understand about

Web sites and the skills they needed to practice. She carefully prepared the packet so that students would not just jump into the "hands-on" assignments without really developing a sound, conceptual understanding.

To provide students with more involvement in their learning, Mrs. Rowe used contracts. One section of the contract addressed the skills needed for creating a Web site (e.g., choosing a Web site background, identifying the sounds, developing links). The other section of the contract identified what the students needed to know or understand (e.g., What is html? Who needs a Web site? How do the links work?)

As the students worked on each section of their contracts, they would check periodically with Mrs. Rome to discuss what they had learned or to modify the time lines in their contract.

Research and Theory on Providing Feedback

One of the most generalizable strategies a teacher can use is to provide students with feedback relative to how well they are doing. In fact, feedback seems to work well in so many situations that it led researcher John Hattie (1992) to make the following comment after analyzing almost 8,000 studies:

> The most powerful single modification that enhances achievement is feedback. The simplest prescription for improving education must be "dollops of feedback" (p. 9).

Figure 8.2 reports findings from some of the studies that have attempted to synthe-

size research in the general effects of feedback.

We have drawn the following generalizations to guide the use of feedback.

1. Feedback should be "corrective" in nature. Note that some of the effect sizes reported in Figure 8.2 are .90 and even higher. Generally, feedback that produces these large effect sizes is "corrective" in nature. This means that it provides students with an explanation of what they are doing that is correct and what they are doing that is not correct. Perhaps one of the more interesting findings regarding feedback was reported by Bangert-Downs, Kulik, Kulik, and Morgan (1991). The overall effect size they reported was only .26. Their study, however, focused on feedback that takes the form of a test or, as they refer to it, "test-like events." Figure 8.3 reports their findings.

The findings shown in Figure 8.3 have some rather strong implications for education. Notice that simply telling students that their answer on a test is right or wrong has a negative effect on achievement. Providing students with the correct answer has a moderate effect size (.22). The best feedback appears to involve an explanation as to what is accurate and what is inaccurate in terms of student responses. In addition, asking students to keep working on a task until they succeed appears to enhance achievement.

FIGURE 8.2
Research Results for Providing Feedback

Synthesis Study	Focus	No. of Effect Sizes (ESs)	Ave. ES	Percentile Gain
Lysakowski & Walberg, 1982[a]	General effects of feedback	22	.92	32
		7	.69	25
		3	.83	30
		9	.71	26
Lysakowski & Walberg, 1981[a]	General effects of feedback	39	1.15	37
		19	.49	19
		49	.55	21
		11	.19	7
Walberg, 1999	General effects of feedback	20	.94	33
Tennebaum & Goldring, 1989[a]	General effects of feedback	15	.66	25
		7	.80	29
		3	.52	20
		3	.51	19
		2	.67	25
Bloom, 1976	General effects of feedback	7	.54	21
Scheerens & Bosker, 1997	General effects of feedback	—	1.09	36
Kumar, 1991	General effects of feedback	5	1.35	41
Haller, Child, & Walberg, 1988	General effects of feedback	20	.71	26
Bangert-Downs, Kulik, Kulik, & Morgan, 1991	General effects of feedback	58	.26	10

[a] Multiple effect sizes are listed because of the manner in which effect sizes were reported. Readers should consult those studies for more details.

2. Feedback should be timely. The timing of feedback appears to be critical to its effectiveness. To illustrate, consider Figure 8.4, which is also derived from the Bangert-Drowns study.

Feedback given immediately after a test-like situation is best. In general, the more delay that occurs in giving feedback, the less improvement there is in achievement. Notice that feedback immediately after a test item has a relatively low average effect size of .19, and providing students with feedback immediately after a test has the largest effect size (.72). Finally, consider the different effects for timing of test-like feedback. Giving tests immediately after a learning

FIGURE 8.3

Research Results for Corrective Feedback

Synthesis Study	Focus	No. of Effect Sizes (ESs)	Ave. ES	Percentile Gain
Type of Feedback	Right/wrong answer	6	–.08	–3
	Correct answer	39	.22	9
	Repeat until correct	4	.53	20
	Explanation	9	.53	20

situation has a very negligible effect on achievement. Giving a test one day after a learning situation seems to be optimal.

3. **Feedback should be specific to a criterion.** For feedback to be most useful, it should reference a specific level of skill or knowledge. A different way of saying this is that feedback should be criterion-referenced, as opposed to norm-referenced.

When feedback is norm-referenced, it informs students about where they stand in relationship to other students. This tells students nothing about their learning. Criterion-referenced feedback tells students where they stand relative to a specific target of knowledge or skill. In fact, research has consistently indicated that criterion-referenced feedback has a more powerful

FIGURE 8.4

Timing of Feedback

Synthesis Study	Focus	No. of Effect Sizes (ESs)	Ave. ES	Percentile Gain
Timing of feedback	Immediately after item	49	.19	7
	Immediately after test	2	.72	26
	Delayed after test	8	.56	21
Timing of test	Immediately	37	.17	6
	One day	2	.74	27
	One week	12	.53	20
	Longer	4	.26	10

effect on student learning than norm-referenced feedback (see Crooks, 1988; Wilburn & Felps, 1983).

4. Students can effectively provide some of their own feedback. We tend to think that providing feedback is something done exclusively by teachers. Research indicates, however, that students can effectively monitor their own progress (see Trammel, Schloss, & Alper, 1994). Commonly, this takes the form of students' simply keeping track of their performance as learning occurs (see Lindsley, 1972). For example, students might keep a chart of their accuracy, their speed, or both while learning a new skill. The use of student feedback in the form of self-evaluation has been strongly advocated by researcher Grant Wiggins (1993), and its utility in the classroom demonstrated by classroom teachers (see Countryman & Schroeder, 1996).

Classroom Practice in Providing Feedback

Criterion-Referenced Feedback

The manner in which students receive feedback is important for student achievement. As discussed previously, criterion-referenced feedback is superior to norm-referenced feedback. In nontechnical terms, this means that providing students with feedback in terms of specific levels of knowledge and skill is better than simply providing students with a percentage score. One powerful set of tools to this end is rubrics. Figure 8.5A provides a general rubric for content that is more informational in nature. Figure 8.5B is a rubric for content that is more process oriented.

Teachers can adapt these generic rubrics to specific content. Figure 8.6A shows how a teacher has adapted the generic rubric for *information* to the topic of the Industrial Revolution. Figure 8.6B shows how a teacher has adapted the generic rubric for *processes and skills* to reading a bar graph.

Feedback for Specific Types of Knowledge and Skill

In general, the more specific feedback is, the better. When possible, teachers should try to focus their feedback on specific types of knowledge and skill. The following example shows how a high school teacher came to realize the importance of specific feedback.

Mr. Cordova overheard some of his students in the hallway talking about the essays they had turned in for Mrs. McQueen's class: "Mrs. McQueen takes about six weeks to get our papers back to us. I don't even remember what I wrote about by the time she gets it back to me. If she gave them back the next day, I could actually *learn* something from her comments. This way, I just stuff it in

FIGURE 8.5

Rubrics for Providing Feedback

Scale: 4 = excellent; 3 = good; 2 = needs improvement; 1 = unacceptable; 0 = no judgment possible

A: General Rubric for Information

4   The student has a complete and detailed understanding of the information important to the topic.

3   The student has a complete understanding of the information important to the topic but not in great detail.

2   The student has an incomplete understanding of the topic and/or misconceptions about some of the information. However, the student maintains a basic understanding of the topic.

1   The student's understanding of the topic is so incomplete or has so many misconceptions that the student cannot be said to understand the topic.

0   No judgment can be made about the student's understanding of the topic.

B: Generic Rubric for Processes and Skills

4   The student can perform the skill or process important to the topic with no significant errors and with fluency. Additionally, the student understands the key features of the process.

3   The student can perform the skill or process important to the topic without making significant errors.

2   The student makes some significant errors when performing the skill or process important to the topic but still accomplishes a rough approximation of the skill or process.

1   The student makes so many errors in performing the skill or process important to the topic that he or she cannot actually perform the skill or process.

0   No judgment can be made about the student's ability to perform the skill or process.

---

my folder. And the worst part is that when she does get it back to me, it's got one grade on it. A 'B' is supposed to mean *what*? Why can't she just give me a grade for how it was written and another grade for whether or not the content was right?"

As he listened to the students, Mr. Cordova got to thinking about the stack of tests that were sitting in his briefcase and his own methods of providing students with feedback. He had promised himself to grade them over the weekend, and now it was already the next Thursday.

The students continued, "Also, I hate it when we have a bunch of questions to an-

swer and they just circle the one that is wrong and sometimes I don't know *what* was wrong. How is that supposed to help?"

"I know. Sometimes it seems like they just want to give us a grade for the paper, but they don't really care if we learn it."

Mr. Cordova vowed to provide students with better feedback. He went back to his class and graded his papers by writing a few comments next to information that was incorrect. The next day when he returned the papers, he shared with students his concern that the feedback he provided was not really helping them learn. He explained that from now on, he was going to give feedback

---

FIGURE 8.6

Rubric Adaptations

Scale: 4 = excellent; 3 = good; 2 = needs improvement; 1 = unacceptable; 0 = no judgment possible

A: Industrial Revolution Rubric—Information

4   The student has a complete and detailed understanding of the information important to the Industrial Revolution.

3   The student has a complete understanding of the information important to the Industrial Revolution but not in great detail.

2   The student has an incomplete understanding of the Industrial Revolution and/or misconceptions about some of the information. However, the student maintains a basic understanding of the topic.

1   The student's understanding of the Industrial Revolution is so incomplete or has so many misconceptions that the student cannot be said to understand the Industrial Revolution.

0   No judgment can be made about the student's understanding of the Industrial Revolution.

B: Reading Bar Graph Rubric—Processes and Skills

4   The student can perform the skills and processes important to reading a bar graph with no significant errors and with fluency. Additionally, the student understands the key feature of the process of reading a bar graph.

3   The student can perform the process of reading a bar graph without making significant errors.

2   The student makes significant errors when performing the process of reading a bar graph but still accomplishes a rough approximation of the process of reading a bar graph.

1   The student makes so many errors in the process of reading a bar graph that he or she cannot actually read a bar graph.

0   No judgment can be made about the student's ability to perform the process of reading a bar graph.

---

about the knowledge and skill they were demonstrating. He then elicited from the students suggestions related to how he could best communicate that feedback. Although a few students didn't really seem to care about anything but the letter grade, Mr. Cordova was impressed that most of them had sincere, thoughtful suggestions for giving better feedback.

Student-Led Feedback

There is no reason why students should not be part of the feedback process. In fact,

student-led feedback has many desirable effects. The following example shows student-led feedback in the context of a social studies class.

Mr. Hunter's high school classes were doing well with their biographies, and he was pleased with their response to his feedback. One day Judy, a very good student, made a suggestion that she thought might work. She recommended that the students trade their drafts when they felt they were ready so that they could give feedback to one another. "It's not that I don't appreciate what you are telling us, Mr. Hunter, it's just that maybe by having a lot of different people read our drafts, we could benefit from the new ideas."

When he asked the class if they liked the idea, they agreed. Richelle also suggested that she wanted to be able to identify the places where she needed some help so that when she did get feedback, it was specific to the area where she felt she was having problems. "I think that it is a good idea to get some re-action to my biography in draft form," she said, "but I'd like to be able to pinpoint where I think the problems are. I just don't want to be bombarded with a lot of new ideas if I can't fix what I'm working on right now."

Mr. Hunter agreed to schedule class time for student-led feedback.

♦ ♦ ♦

Although common practice in most K–12 classrooms, setting objectives and providing feedback are frequently underused in terms of their flexibility and power. In this chapter, we have explored a number of options within both of these categories of instructional strategies.

9

GENERATING AND TESTING HYPOTHESES

Tisha, a 2nd grader, stared up at the sky for a long time and then announced, "I think we are going to have a bad storm. It was hot, but now feel how cold it is and look at those cumulus clouds." Her grandma stared in amazement. "Aren't you the weather girl today! Where did you learn all that?" Tisha explained that her teacher had been discussing weather with them all year.

"Our teacher said that weather was there for us to study all year, so why study it all at once and then probably forget it? She said we weren't just going to learn it, we were going to use what we learned. Besides, it means we get to go outside to learn."

Tisha's teacher periodically taught her students about specific weather patterns. Approximately once every two weeks, the class would look at a weather map on the Internet, discuss what had been happening during the last 24 hours, then go outside and observe the sky, once in the morning and once in the afternoon. The students would then predict what they thought would happen between the end of the school day and the next morning. They would also explain the reasoning behind their predictions.

During the first few minutes of the following morning, students discussed their hypotheses and the extent to which they were correct. If their predictions were accurate, they identified the observations that helped them the most. If their predictions were inaccurate, students tried to figure out what they missed or misunderstood.

Tisha's teacher has used the topic of weather to engage students in one of the most powerful and analytic of cognitive operations—generating and testing hypotheses.

Research and Theory on Generating and Testing Hypotheses

By definition, the process of generating and testing hypotheses involves the application of knowledge. It is something we do quite naturally in many situations (see Hansell, 1988; Heller & Reif, 1984; Koedinger & Anderson, 1993; Koedinger & Tabachneck, 1994). For example, a student is involved in generating and testing hypotheses if, after watching a demonstration of how air flow travels over the wing of an airplane, he concludes that changing the shape of the wing in a specific way will have a specific effect on the flow of air. The student would then actually design a wing with the desired shape and then test his conjecture. Figure 9.1 summarizes some of the research on this general category of instructional strategy.

Two generalizations can guide the use of hypothesis generation and testing in the classroom.

1. Hypothesis generation and testing can be approached in a more inductive or deductive manner. Deductive thinking is the process of using a general rule to make a prediction about a future action or event (see Johnson-Laird, 1983). For example, while beginning to read a story about a particular wolf, you will naturally access some of the generalizations you have about wolves from your permanent memory. If one of those generalizations is "Wolves run in packs and are highly social," then you will predict that the story will contain episodes about the interaction of the individual wolf with other wolves that are members of a pack.

Inductive thinking, on the other hand, is the process of drawing new conclusions based on information we know or are

FIGURE 9.1

Research Results for Generating and Testing Hypotheses

Synthesis Study	Focus	No. of Effect Sizes (ESs)	Ave. ES	Percentile Gain
Hattie et al., 1996	General effects of generating and testing hypotheses	2	.79	28
Lott, 1983	General effects of generating and testing hypotheses	22	.04	2
Ross, 1988	General effects of generating and testing hypotheses	104	.72	26

presented with (see Holland, Holyoak, Nisbett, & Thagard, 1986). For example, if you are reading an account of how a particular bear behaved when being observed by a scientist, you would induce that the behaviors the scientist had frequently observed are behaviors the bear habitually engages in, or even behaviors that all bears habitually engage in. It is worth noting that thinking in real life is probably never purely inductive or deductive. Rather, scholars assert that reasoning is often more "messy" and nonlinear than earlier definitions suggest (Deely, 1982; Eco, 1976, 1979, 1984; Medawar, 1967; Percy, 1975).

Inductive instructional techniques require students to first discover the principles from which hypotheses are generated. In the air flow example, a teacher would be using an inductive approach if she asked students first to discover principles about air flow and then to generate hypotheses based on these discovered principles. A teacher would be using a deductive approach, however, if she first presented students with principles of air flow, such as the Bernoulli theorem. With this knowledge as a basis, she would then ask students to generate and test hypotheses based on the principles they have been taught. Although both inductive and deductive approaches can work well, generally speaking, deductive approaches produce better results. To illustrate, consider the research findings in Figure 9.2.

As reported in the last two rows of Figure 9.2, the average effect size for deductive techniques is much larger than that for inductive techniques (.60 versus .39). This is not to say that inductive approaches cannot produce large effect sizes. Perhaps teachers find inductive approaches more difficult to execute correctly. Inductive strategies require a well-orchestrated set of experiences so that students might infer accurate and appropriate principles from which to generate hypotheses. In the absence of experiences that allow students to do this, it is probably better to present principles directly to students and then ask them to generate hypotheses.

2. Teachers should ask students to clearly explain their hypotheses and their conclusions. A fair amount of research has demonstrated the power of asking students to carefully explain—preferably in writing—the principles they are working from, the hypotheses they generate from these principles, and why their hypotheses make sense (see Lavoie, 1999; Lavoie & Good, 1988; Lawson, 1988). Apparently, the process of explaining their thinking helps students deepen their understanding of the principles they are applying. If an inductive approach is being used, students might be asked to explain the logic underlying their observations, how their observations support their hypotheses, how their experiment tests their hypotheses, and how their results confirm or disconfirm their hypotheses. If a deductive technique is being

FIGURE 9.2

Inductive versus Deductive Approaches

Synthesis Study	Focus	No. of Effect Sizes (ESs)	Ave. ES	Percentile Gain
Tamir, 1985	Deductive techniques	13	.27	11
Lott, 1983	Deductive techniques	18	.02	1
	Inductive techniques	4	.10	4
El-Nemr, 1980	Inductive techniques	250	.38	15
Sweitzer & Anderson, 1983	Inductive techniques	19	.43	17
Walberg, 1999	Inductive techniques	38	.41	16
Ross, 1988	Inductive techniques	39	.48	19
	Deductive techniques	65	.83	30
Average ES for inductive techniques		380	.39	15
Average ES for deductive techniques		96	.60	23

used, students would not be engaged in the observation phase of this process.

Classroom Practice in Generating and Testing Hypotheses

Using a Variety of Structured Tasks to Guide Students Through Generating and Testing Hypotheses

Although the process of generating and testing hypotheses is commonly associated with the scientific method, teachers can use the process in different tasks across all disciplines. The following six types of tasks all employ hypotheses generation and testing.

Systems Analysis. Students at all grade levels study many systems across the disciplines, such as ecosystems, anatomical systems, systems of government, and transportation systems. One way to enhance and use students' understanding of these systems is to ask them to generate hypotheses that predict what would happen if some aspect of a system were changed. The following general framework for systems analysis might be useful in guiding students' work.

1. Explain the purpose of the system, the parts of the system, and the function of each part.

2. Describe how the parts affect each other.

3. Identify a part of the system, describe a change in that part, and then hypothesize what would happen as a result of this change.

4. When possible, test your hypothesis by actually changing the part or by using a simulation to change the part.

Problem Solving. By definition, problems involve obstacles and constraints. While engaged in solving problems, students must generate and test hypotheses related to the various solutions they predict might work. For example, a teacher might present students with a task that requires them to build something (e.g., a model car, a bridge) under the constraint that they are allowed to use limited or specific materials only (e.g., balsa wood, a rubber band, a mousetrap). Using their understanding of concepts related to the problem (e.g., inertia, gravity, energy, force, and motion) they must consider different approaches to a solution and then generate and test their hypotheses about those solutions. Students might use the following general framework to guide their work.

1. Identify the goal you are trying to accomplish.

2. Describe the barriers or constraints that are preventing you from achieving your goal—that are creating the problem.

3. Identify different solutions for overcoming the barriers or constraints and hypothesize which solution is likely to work.

4. Try your solution—either in reality or through a simulation.

5. Explain whether your hypothesis was correct. Determine if you want to test another hypothesis using a different solution.

Historical Investigation. Students are engaged in historical investigation when they construct plausible scenarios for events from the past, about which there is no general agreement. For example, scholars have presented conflicting versions of Roosevelt's role in the events that led up to the bombing of Pearl Harbor. To engage in historical investigation, students need to use their understanding of the situation to generate a hypothetical scenario. To test this hypothesis, each student must then seek out and analyze as much information as possible to determine if the hypothesis is supported by the evidence. Students might use the following general framework for historical investigation:

1. Clearly describe the historical event to be examined.

2. Identify what is known or agreed on and what is not known or about which there is disagreement.

3. Based on what you understand about the situation, offer a hypothetical scenario.

4. Seek out and analyze evidence to determine if your hypothetical scenario is plausible.

Invention. Another task that requires students to generate and test hypotheses is the process of invention. For example, students might use their understanding of the principles of the cardiovascular and muscular system to invent a new form of exercise. To do this, they must hypothesize what might work, develop the idea, and then conduct tests to determine if their idea does, in fact, work. Invention often demands generating and testing multiple hypotheses, until one of them proves effective. As students engage in invention, they might use the following general framework as a guide:

1. Describe a situation you want to improve or a need to which you want to respond.

2. Identify specific standards for the invention that would improve the situation or would meet the need.

3. Brainstorm ideas and hypothesize the likelihood that they will work.

4. When your hypothesis suggests that a specific idea might work, begin to draft, sketch, or actually create the invention.

5. Develop your invention to the point where you can test your hypothesis.

6. If necessary, revise your invention until it reaches the standards you have set.

Experimental Inquiry. We most commonly associate the process of experimental inquiry with generating and testing hypotheses in science. But teachers can use experimental inquiry across the disciplines to guide students in applying their understanding of important content. For example, based on their understanding of how literary devices in literature have influenced readers, students might hypothesize the effects of using specific literary devices in their own writing. Teachers might use the following general framework to help students engage in any experimental inquiry task:

1. Observe something of interest to you and describe what you observe.

2. Apply specific theories or rules to explain what you have observed.

3. Based on your explanation, generate a hypothesis to predict what would happen if you applied the theories or rules to what you observed or to a situation related to what you observed.

4. Set up an experiment or engage in an activity to test your hypothesis.

5. Explain the results of your experiment or activity. Decide if your hypothesis was correct and if you need to conduct additional experiments or activities or if you need to generate and test an alternative hypothesis.

Decision Making. Although we might not associate decision with generating and testing hypotheses, using a structured decision-making framework can help students examine hypothetical situations, especially those requiring them to select what has the *most* or *least* of something or what is the *best* or *worst* example of something. For example, if students were asked to predict who is the most influential musical group or visual artist of the last decade, many students would quickly offer a prediction. If they were then asked to test this hypothesis by using a structured decision-making framework, the result might be different from what they predicted. Further, using a decision-making process to test their prediction requires them to reflect on and use a broad range of knowledge related to the topic. Students might use the following framework to guide them through such decision making tasks:

1. Describe the decision you are making and the alternatives you are considering.

2. Identify the criteria that will influence the selection and indicate the relative importance of the criteria by assigning an importance score from a designated scale, for example, 1–4.

3. Rate each alternative on a designated scale (e.g., 1–4) to indicate the extent to which each alternative meets each criterion.

4. For each alternative, multiply the importance score and the rating and then add the products to assign a score for the alternative.

5. Examine the scores to determine the alternative with the highest score.

6. Based on your reaction to the selected alternative, determine if you need to change any importance scores or add or drop criteria.

The following example shows how teachers can use more than one of these processes within a single topic.

> Mr. Sanders wanted to present his 10th grade students with a variety of ways to test and generate hypotheses in his unit on World War II. After teaching the students some basic facts and issues about the war, he asked them to select one of the following projects:
>
> **Decision Making.** What is your hypothesis as to the best method of ending World War II other than the use of the atomic bomb? Use the decision-making framework to test your hypothesis.
>
> **Problem Solving.** If you were president of the United States during World War II, how would you force the unconditional surrender of Japan without using the atomic bomb and yet provide for a secure, post-war world?
>
> **Investigation.** Why did Japan attack Pearl Harbor? Some say President Roosevelt intentionally provoked the Japanese. Others disagree. What is your hypothesis? Collect evidence that confirms this hypothesis.

Making Sure Students Can Explain Their Hypotheses and Their Conclusions

The second generalization in this category of instructional strategies reminds us to ask students to explain their thinking as they generate and test hypotheses. Teachers can design assignments so that students know they must be able to describe how they generated their hypotheses and to explain what they learned as a result of testing them. For example, a teacher might

• Provide students with templates for reporting their work, highlighting the areas in which they will be expected to provide explanations.

• Provide sentence stems for students, especially for young students, to help them articulate their explanations.

• Ask students to turn in audiotapes on which they explain their hypotheses and conclusions.

• Provide, or develop with students, rubrics so that they know that the criteria on which they will be evaluated are based on the quality of their explanations.

• Set up events during which parents or community members ask students to explain their thinking.

The following example shows how an art teacher might design assignments that require students to explain how they generated and tested hypotheses.

The 5th grade art teacher had finally found a way for students to demonstrate and enhance their understanding of how the elements of a painting work together as a system (e.g., color influences the impact of perspective and is influenced by texture, etc.). Through a projection system connected to her computer, she projected a famous painting on the screen in front of the classroom. She then told the students that she could change a single element (color, depth, contrast) with the computer. Before she changed each element, the students, working in pairs, were asked to predict how they thought changing one element would influence the impact of the other elements. She then made the suggested change and allowed students time to react. After each change, she selected students to explain to the class what they predicted the effect would be, why their prediction was logical, and the extent to which their prediction was confirmed or disconfirmed.

◆ ◆ ◆

We commonly think of generating and testing hypotheses as the purview of the science teacher only. As this chapter has shown, this basic cognitive skill applies to a variety of tasks that are applicable to many subject areas.

10

CUES, QUESTIONS, AND ADVANCE ORGANIZERS

At the beginning of an introductory high school psychology course, Mrs. Crawford writes the word *psychology* on the board. Then she asks students to tell her everything they know about the term. As students answer, she writes key words on the board. Mrs. Crawford selects a few words to consider in more depth—*Freud, psychoanalysis, ego, id, bipolar, multiple personalities.* For each selected item, students are asked what they know to be true or believe to be true. When she asks students what they know about Sigmund Freud, she is surprised at the depth of their knowledge about him. As students address each term, Mrs. Crawford records ideas on the board. By the end of the discussion, Mrs. Crawford has a list of the basic knowledge students have about psychology. Throughout the course, Mrs. Crawford uses this information as the springboard for introducing new information.

The techniques in the final category of instructional strategies all help students retrieve what they already know about a topic. In nontechnical terms, this is sometimes referred to as "activating prior knowledge." Mrs. Crawford was activating the prior knowledge of her students in an informal but effective way.

Educational researchers have shown that the activation of prior knowledge is critical to learning of all types. Indeed, our background knowledge can even influence what we perceive. Brewer and Treyens (1981) demonstrated this effect. They brought 30 students individually into a room and told them that it was the office of a professor who was conducting an experiment. Each student was asked to wait for a short while. After 35 seconds, the students were taken to another room and asked to write down everything they could recall about the office. Brewer and Tryens hypothesized that students would remember those items they *expected* to see in a professor's office, regardless of whether they were there or not. In other words, the researchers hypothesized that students' prior knowledge would actually influence what they perceived. This is precisely what happened. Specifically, 29 of 30 students remembered that the office had a desk and a chair, but only 8 recalled that it had a bulletin board and a skull; and 9 students recalled that the office had books—which it did not. The students remembered what they expected to see, regardless of whether it was there or not. Use of prior knowledge can be a powerful learning tool. Cues and questions, as well as advance organizers, are techniques that call on students' prior knowledge.

Research and Theory on Cues and Questions

Cues and questions are ways that a classroom teacher helps students use what they already know about a topic. Figure 10.1 summarizes findings from some of the studies that have attempted to synthesize the research on cues and questions.

Although Figure 10.1 distinguishes between cues and questions, the two techniques are similar. Cues involve "hints" about what students are about to experi-

FIGURE 10.1
Research Results for Cues and Questions

Synthesis Study	Focus	No. of Effect Sizes (ESs)	Ave. ES	Percentile Gain
Ross, 1988	Cues	6	.41	16
Walberg, 1999	Questions	14	.26	10
Redfield & Rousseau, 1981	Questions	7	.73	27
Wise & Okey, 1983	Questions	5	.37	14
	Cues	38	.53	20
Stone, 1983	Cues	83	.75	27
Bloom, 1976	Cues	11	1.21	39
Crismore, 1985	Cues	231	.60	23
Hamaker, 1986	Questions	100	.75	27
Guzzetti, Snyder, & Glass, 1993	Cues and Questions	11	.80	29

ence. For example, a teacher is providing students with a cue when she explains that the film they are about to watch on the functioning of the cell will present some information they already know about the cell, but it will also provide some new information. Because the teacher provided the topic of the film for students, she allowed them to activate their prior knowledge. Also, the teacher has told them to expect some new information, which establishes expectations for students. Questions perform about the same function. For example, before watching the film on the functioning of the cell, the teacher might ask students questions that elicit what they already know about the topic.

It is probably safe to say that cueing and questioning are at the heart of classroom practice. In fact, research in classroom behavior indicates that cueing and questioning might account for as much as 80 percent of what occurs in a given classroom on a given day (see Davis, O. L., & Tinsley, 1967; Fillippone, 1998). In addition, teachers are largely unaware of the extent to which they use cueing and questioning. To illustrate, in a study published in 1974, Nash and Shiman found that elementary teachers who thought they were asking 12 to 20 questions every half hour were actually asking 45 to 150 questions. Fillippone (1998) has reported this same trend in recent years.

The following generalizations can guide teachers in using cues and questions:

1. **Cues and questions should focus on what is important as opposed to what is unusual.** Several studies have demonstrated that all too often teachers structure questions around information that is unusual or that they perceive as interesting, as opposed to information that is critical to the topic being studied (see Alexander & Judy, 1988; Alexander, Kulikowich, & Schulze, 1994; Risner, Nicholson, & Webb, 1994). Many teachers engage in this practice under the mistaken assumption that it will increase students' interest in the topic. What is ironic about this situation is that research actually indicates that the more students know about a topic, the more they tend to be interested in it (Alexander et al., 1994). Consequently, questions designed to help students obtain a deeper understanding of content will eventually increase their interest in the topic.

2. **"Higher level" questions produce deeper learning than "lower level" questions.** A fair amount of research indicates that questions that require students to analyze information—frequently called higher-level questions—produce more learning than questions that simply require students to recall or recognize information—frequently referred to as lower-order questions (see Redfield & Rousseau, 1981). Unfortunately, most of the questions teachers ask are lower order in nature (Davis, O. L., & Tinsley, 1967; Fillippone, 1998; Guszak, 1967; Mueller, 1973). Although you can find many definitions of

higher-level questions, they all have the common feature of requiring students to restructure information or apply knowledge in some way.

3. **"Waiting" briefly before accepting responses from students has the effect of increasing the depth of students' answers.** Closely related to questioning is the use of "wait time." Expanding on Rowe's (1974) original definition of wait time as pausing for several seconds after asking a question to give students time to think before being called on to answer, Tobin (1987) identified a number of different types of wait time (e.g., the pause following any teacher's utterance and any student utterance, the pause following any student utterance and preceding any teacher utterance). Given its simplicity and ease of execution, wait time appears to be a highly useful instructional technique. Researchers have found it to be associated with such noteworthy aspects of learning as more student discourse (Swift & Gooding, 1983) and more student-to-student interaction (Fowler, 1975; Honea, 1982).

4. **Questions are effective learning tools even when asked before a learning experience.** We generally think of questioning as something teachers do *after* students have been engaged in a learning experience—watching a demonstration, reading, listening to a lecture. Teachers, however, can use questions *before* a learning experience to establish a "mental set" with which students process the learning experience.

Again, higher-level questions tend to produce deeper levels of learning (Hamaker, 1986; Osman & Hannafin, 1994; Pressley et al., 1988; Pressley, Tenebaum, McDaniel, & Wood, 1990; Pressley et al., 1992).

Classroom Practice in Cues and Questions

Explicit Cues

Cues are straightforward ways of activating prior knowledge. Using cues, teachers can provide students with a preview of what they are about to experience. The following example shows the use of cues in an elementary school Spanish class.

> Sra. Nina starts her 3rd grade class by asking if anyone has a friend who is known for borrowing things. Those people, she says, are called "pediguenos" in Spanish, or "leeches" in English. Sra. Nina then explains:
> "We dedicate our lesson today to the *pediguenos* because we are going to learn how to use possessive adjectives, or *adjetivos posesivos*. We will learn and practice the possessive adjectives for you, *tu, el, ella, Ud., nosotros, vosotros, ellos, ellas, y Uds*. For example, Peter doesn't use his own car; he borrows his friend's car. Now let's say it in Spanish."

Questions That Elicit Inferences

Even the best-designed lesson will demand that students "fill in" a great deal of missing information. Questions can greatly aid students in this process. Teachers might use the following questions to help students make inferences about things, people, actions, events, and states of being they might be studying.

Things/People:

What action does this thing or person usually perform?

What action is usually performed on this thing?

How is this thing usually used?

What is this thing part of?

What is the process for making this thing?

Does this thing have a particular taste, feel, smell, sound? What is it?

Does this thing have a particular color, number (or quantity), location, or dimensionality? What is it?

How is this thing usually sold?

Does this thing have a particular emotional state? What is it?

Does this thing have a particular value?

When this thing is used, does it present a particular danger to other things or to people? What is it?

Actions:

What thing or person usually performs this action?

What effect does this action have on the taste, feel, sound, or look of this thing?

How does this action typically change the emotional state of a thing or person?

How is the value of a thing changed by this action?

How does this action change the size or shape of a thing?

How does this action change the state of a thing?

Events:

What people are usually involved in this event?

During what season or time of year does this event usually take place?

On what day of the week does this event usually take place?

At what time of day does this event usually take place?

Where does this event usually take place?

At what point in history did this event take place?

What equipment is typically used in this event?

How long does this event usually take?

States (of Being):

What is the basic process involved in reaching this state?

What are the changes that occur when something reaches this state?

To use these questions, a teacher would identify things, people, actions, events, and states in information the students were learning and then ask questions, modeled on the preceding examples, about these identified elements. The following example shows how a teacher used such questions in the context of a health class.

> After her 6th grade students were finished reading an article about different eating disorders, Mrs. Conzone presented them with some inferential questions to help clarify issues in the article. Two questions were:
>
> 1. What actions do these individuals perform?
> 2. What actions are usually performed on these individuals?
>
> One of the students answered the questions in the following way:
>
> 1. *What actions do these individuals perform?* I thought people with eating disorders were those people who did not eat, but is the definition a broader one? In other words, is a person who overeats considered one with an eating disorder?
> 2. *What actions are usually performed on these individuals?* It seems that each one of the disorders can stem from a different kind of problem, so the diagnosis and prescription has to be very individualized.

Analytic Questions

Some questions require students to analyze and even critique the information presented to them. To facilitate this type of questioning, it is useful to have a list of analytic skills (see Figure 10.2).

Each type of analysis listed in Figure 10.2 can be cued by one or more specific questions like the following:

Analyzing Errors:

What are the errors in reasoning in this information?

How is this information misleading?

How could it be corrected or improved?

Constructing Support:

What is an argument that would support the following claim?

What are some of the limitations of this argument or the assumptions underlying it?

Analyzing Perspectives:

Why would someone consider this to be good (or bad or neutral)?

What is the reasoning behind his or her perspective?

What is an alternative perspective, and what is the reasoning behind it?

The following example shows how one teacher used these questions in the context of a middle school science class.

> During a unit on physical environments of the world, Ms. Egan asks students to design

---

FIGURE 10.2

Definition of Analytic Skills

Analyzing Errors: Identifying and articulating errors in the logic of information.

Constructing Support: Constructing a system of support or proof for an assertion.

Analyzing Perspectives: Identifying and articulating personal perspectives about issues.

an argument for or against the protection of "old growth" forests. Regardless of the position they take, students are required to present a sound argument and are judged on the strength of their argument and the strength of their evidence.

Research and Theory on Advance Organizers

Another way that teachers can help students use their background knowledge to learn new information is to present them with advance organizers. The concept of advance organizers was first popularized by psychologist David Ausubel (1968), who defined them in the following way:

Appropriately relevant and inclusive introductory materials ... introduced in advance of learning ... and presented at a higher level of abstraction, generality, and inclusiveness than the information presented after it. The organizer serves to provide ideational scaffolding for the stable incorporation and retention of the more detailed and differentiated materials that follow. Thus, advance organizers are not the same as summaries or overviews, which comprise text at the same level of abstraction as the material to be learned, but rather are designed to bridge the gap between what the learner already knows and what he needs to know before he can successfully learn the task at hand (p. 148).

Since Ausubel's first writings on the topic, researchers have studied advance organizers in great depth. Figure 10.3 summarizes the

FIGURE 10.3				
Research Results for Advance Organizers				
Synthesis Study	**Focus**	**No. of Effect Sizes (ESs)**	**Ave. ES**	**Percentile Gain**
Walberg, 1999	General effects of advance organizers	29 16	.45 .24	17 9
Hattie, 1992	General effects of advance organizers	387	.37	14
Lott, 1983[a]	General effects of advance organizers	17 5	.09 .77	3 28
Stone, 1983	Expository advance organizers	44	.80	29
	Narrative advance organizers	12	.53	20
	Skimming as an advance organizer	15	.71	26
	Illustrated advance organizers	15	.52	20

[a] Two effect sizes are listed for the Lott study because of the manner in which effect sizes were reported. Readers should consult that study for more details.

findings from some of the studies that have attempted to synthesize the research on advance organizers.

Advance organizers are closely related to cues and questions. Indeed, the fourth generalization pertaining to cues and questions addresses questions as advance organizers. Consequently, many of the generalizations that apply to cues and questions also apply to advance organizers. Specifically, consider the following:

1. **Advance organizers should focus on what is important as opposed to what is unusual.**

2. **"Higher level" advance organizers produce deeper learning than the "lower level" advance organizers.**

Because we discussed these generalizations in the previous section, we will not address them here. Research studies specific to advance organizers, however, imply some other generalizations, as follows:

3. **Advance organizers are most useful with information that is not well organized.** Since advance organizers, by definition, provide students with a way of organizing information implicit or explicit within a learning experience, it is no wonder that they have more powerful effects with information that is organized poorly than with information that is well organized (see Martorella, 1991; Mayer, 1979; White & Tisher, 1986). For example, an advance organizer might work better as a preparation for a field trip than it would as a preparation for reading a chapter in a textbook that is well organized with clear headings and subheadings.

4. **Different types of advance organizers produce different results.** As Figure 10.3 shows, there are four general types of advance organizers—expository, narrative, skimming, and illustrated. All produce fairly powerful results, but of the four, expository has the largest effect size. These four are not the only types of advance organizers. These findings point out, however, that advance organizers come in many different formats.

Classroom Practice in Advance Organizers

Expository Advance Organizers

Expository advance organizers simply describe the new content to which students are to be exposed. The following example shows its use in the context of a middle school unit on careers.

Although the Career Day team had prepared a nice agenda, it lacked any information about how to learn best from the different speakers that would visit throughout the day. In preparation, Mr. Matamoros created an advance organizer for his students. The organizer included a series of brief explanations about each career that would be presented. Mr. Matamoros had students read each description. Then, as a whole class, they briefly discussed each career. Mr. Matamoros told students to consult the information contained in the advance organizers as they heard about each career option.

After Career Day, many of the students commented that they felt that the organizer was critical to their understanding of the information about the various careers. Some of the visitors who led the sessions expressed the fact that they were impressed with the quality and focus of students' questions.

Narrative Advance Organizers

Narrative advance organizers present information to students in story format. The following example shows how one teacher used a narrative advance organizer with the topic of tornadoes.

> Before Ms. Neeley's 4th grade class viewed a film about tornadoes, she told them this personal story about tornadoes:
>
> "I was in a tornado once, but I didn't know it until after it was over! I had gone to visit my sister. It was 3:00 in the afternoon, and we were in the living room drinking tea and talking. It became very dark, and it was only 3:00 in the afternoon! But we never dreamed a tornado was coming. We just turned on the lights, opened the window shades, and continued to drink tea and talk. A bit later the lights suddenly went out and, at the same time, sirens started wailing. We kind of wondered what was going on, but it didn't occur to us to worry. A few minutes later my husband called—the phones were still working. He asked me if I was okay and I said, "Of course, why wouldn't I be?" He told me that a tornado had just touched

down about four blocks from where I was. Suddenly it all made sense. My sister and I raced down the street, and sure enough, the tornado had cut a path right through an intersection. The stop lights were upside down, cars were overturned, and huge trees had been uprooted. The glass was blown out of the windows at a furniture store and across the street at a fast food restaurant. The destruction was awesome."

Skimming as a Form of Advance Organizer

Skimming information before reading can be a powerful form of advance organizer. The following example shows how a 6th grade teacher used skimming in the context of a science class.

> The students in the 6th grade were going to take a field trip to the Planetarium. For homework, Mr. Armstrong asked the students to skim two pages he reprinted from the Atlas. One was a diagram of the Star Maps of the Northern Hemisphere and the second was the Southern Hemisphere. The maps also had a key and some facts.
>
> "Just skim the maps," he said. "Try to become familiar with some of the patterns so that when we go to the planetarium, you'll have some sense of what you might be seeing."

Graphic Advance Organizers

Chapter 6 discussed graphic organizers as a type of nonlinguistic representation. They also can be effectively used as advance organizers. The following example shows how a teacher used a graphic orga-

FIGURE 10.4

Graphic Organizer: French Class

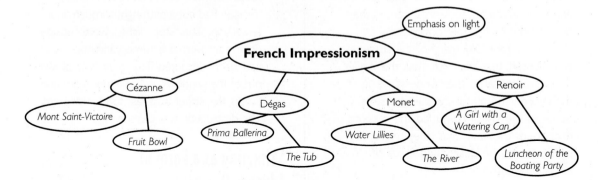

nizer as an advance organizer in an 11th grade French class.

Ms. Hougham wanted to introduce her French students to the French Impressionist painters. Prior to showing them a slide show containing a number of artist's works, she presented her students with a graphic organizer identifying some of the painters to whom they were about to be introduced and some of their works (see Figure 10.4).

She encouraged her students to listen for additional information to add to the graphic organizer—key features of impressionism, perhaps other painters, paintings, or important details about either.

♦ ♦ ♦

Helping students think about new knowledge before experiencing it can go a long way toward enhancing student achievement. Teachers can use cues, questions, and advance organizers to facilitate this type of thinking in a variety of ways and formats.

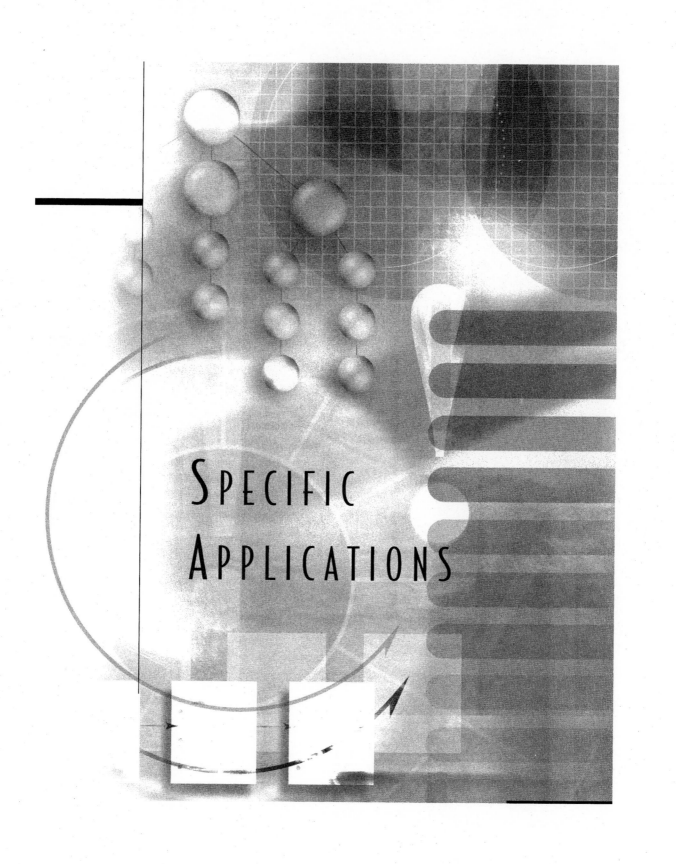

SPECIFIC APPLICATIONS

11

TEACHING SPECIFIC
TYPES OF KNOWLEDGE

In general, the nine categories of instructional strategies described in Chapters 2–10 work well with all types of subject-matter knowledge. If a teacher wishes, however, she can match specific instructional strategies to specific types of knowledge. This notion that different types of knowledge involve different types of learning and, therefore, different types of teaching is not new. Noted educator Ralph Tyler probably introduced it in the 1950s (see *Educational Evaluation: Classic Works of Ralph Tyler* by Madaus & Stufflebeam, 1989). Later, educational reformer Hilda Taba (1962) expanded on this notion, identifying specific instructional strategies for specific types of knowledge.

One can organize subject-matter knowledge into five broad categories: (1) vocabulary terms and phrases, (2) details, (3) organizing ideas, (4) skills and tactics, and (5) processes. The first three cate-gories are informational in nature and are sometimes referred to as "declarative knowledge." The last two categories are more process oriented and are sometimes referred to as "procedural knowledge."

Research and Theory on Vocabulary Terms and Phrases

One of the most generalizable findings in the research is the strong relationship between vocabulary and several important factors, such as

◆ *Intelligence* (Davis, F. B., 1944; Spearitt, 1972; Thorndike & Lorge, 1943).
◆ *One's ability to comprehend new information* (Chall, 1958; Harrison, 1980).
◆ *One's level of income* (Stitcht, Hofstetter, & Hofstetter, 1997).

Given the apparent importance of vocabulary development, one might assume that systematic vocabulary instruction is a critical aspect of the instruction in virtually every school. In fact, some researchers have concluded that systematic vocabulary instruction is one of the most important instructional interventions that teachers can use, particularly with low-achieving students (see Becker, 1977).

It is safe to say, however, that systematic vocabulary instruction is rare in U.S. schools (see McKeown & Curtis, 1987). Moreover, some writers have taken the position that systematic vocabulary instruction is a futile or, at best, a low-yield endeavor in terms of student learning.

The primary argument for this negative position deals with the number of words in the English language. Specifically, Nagy and his colleagues (Nagy & Anderson, 1984; Nagy & Herman, 1984) estimate that the number of words in "printed school English" (i.e., those words K–12 students will encounter in print) is about 85,000. Quite obviously, it would be impossible to teach so many words one at a time. For Nagy and his colleagues, these facts render systematic vocabulary instruction impractical. Stahl and Fairbanks (1986) have summarized Nagy's logic as follows:

> Since a vocabulary teaching program typically teaches 10 to 12 words a week or about 400 words a year, of which perhaps 75% or 300 are learned, vocabulary instruction is not adequate to cope with the volume of new words that children need to learn and do learn without instruction (Stahl & Fairbanks, 1986, p. 100).

Nagy and Herman (1987) offer an alternative to direct vocabulary instruction. They argue:

> If students were to spend 25 minutes a day reading at a rate of 200 words per minute for 200 days out of the year, they would read a million words of text annually. According to our estimates, with this amount of reading, children will encounter between 15,000 and 30,000 unfamiliar words. If one in 20 of these words is learned, the yearly gain in vocabulary will be between 750 and 1,500 words (p. 20).

If one subscribes to their logic, then direct vocabulary instruction is not only ill-advised, but downright foolish. The argument, however, is not entirely accurate. In fact, an analysis of the research provides a strong case for systematic instruction in vocabulary at virtually every grade level.

The following generalizations can be used to guide instruction in vocabulary terms and phrases.

1. Students must encounter words in context more than once to learn them. In part, the conclusion about the utility of wide reading as the primary vehicle for vocabulary development relies on the assumption that students will learn those words they encounter. Wide reading, however, might not add new words to students' vocabularies as easily as one might think.

To illustrate, a study by Jenkins, Stein, and Wysocki (1984) demonstrates that to learn a new word in context (without instruction), students need to be exposed to the word at least six times before they have enough experience with the word to ascertain and remember its meaning. Their research indicates that one or even two exposures to words in context do not produce significant vocabulary learning. In fact, it isn't until exposures reached six that students began to learn and recall new words.

Since the Jenkins and others study, two other major studies have attempted to determine how likely it is for students to learn new words while reading. Where Nagy and Herman (1987) estimated that students have about a 5-percent chance of learning a new word they encountered in their reading, Swanborn and de Glopper (1999) estimated that students have about

a 15-percent chance of learning a new word encountered during reading. Both these studies provide an optimistic view of incidental word learning. But even this optimistic view must be tempered. To illustrate, consider the data in Figure 11.1.

As Figure 11.1 shows, many factors affect the chances that a student will learn new words while reading. High-ability students have a 19-percent chance of learning a new word, whereas low-ability students have an 8-percent chance only. Older students (i.e., grade 11) have a 33-percent chance of learning new words, whereas young students (i.e., grade 4) have an 8-percent chance only. Finally, the nature of text greatly influences the chance that students will learn new words. Low-density text (i.e., 1 new word per 150 words) provides a 30-percent chance that students will learn new words, whereas high-density

---

FIGURE 11.1

Chances of Learning New Words in Context

Characteristic	Factor	Chances of Learning Word
Ability	Low Medium High	8 percent 12 percent 19 percent
Grade Level	Grade 4 Grade 11	8 percent 33 percent
Text Density	for every 10 words for every 74 words for every 150 words	7 percent 14 percent 30 percent

Source: Data from Swanborn & de Glopper, 1999.

text (i.e., 1 new word in 10) provides only a 7-percent chance.

These findings seriously undermine the argument that wide reading is sufficient to enhance the vocabulary development of students, especially when one considers the fact that more than 90 percent of words students encounter in their reading occur less than once in a million words of text; about half occur less than once in a billion words (Nagy & Anderson, 1984).

2. Instruction in new words enhances learning those words in context. Perhaps one of the most useful findings from the Jenkins and others (1984) study is that even superficial instruction on words greatly enhances the probability that students will learn the words from context when they encounter them in their reading. When students have such instruction on words, their ability to comprehend these new words increases by a factor of about one-third. Specifically, students in the Jenkins and others study who had prior instruction on words were about 33 percent more likely to understand new words encountered during reading than did students who had no prior instruction.

What is perhaps most significant about these findings is that the prior instruction the students had was minimal. In fact, instruction amounted simply to providing students with a sheet of paper that contained definitions of the new words, along with an example of each word used in a

sentence. Students were allowed to read the sheet, but they received no help from the teacher. In addition, students had only about 40 seconds to study each word—certainly not enough time to digest the information about these new words in any depth. Yet, even this superficial instruction improved students' chances of understanding these words in context.

3. One of the best ways to learn a new word is to associate an image with it. Numerous studies support the powerful effects of associating mental images or symbolic representations with words being learned. For example, in an analysis of 11 controlled studies, Powell (1980) found that instructional techniques employing the use of imagery produced achievement gains in word knowledge that were 34 percentile points higher than techniques that did not. Figure 11.2 represents the effectiveness of imagery-based techniques as compared with specific types of nonimagery-based instructional methods.

As shown in Figure 11.2, imagery-based techniques produced achievement gains that were 37 percentile points higher than those produced by techniques that focused on having students continually review word definitions. Imagery-based techniques produced achievement gains that were 21 percentile points higher than techniques that focused on having students generate novel sentences that demonstrate an understanding of new words.

FIGURE 11.2

Imagery-Based Instructional Techniques

Methods Compared to Imagery-Based Elaboration	Number of Studies	Percentile Gain for Imagery-Based Elaboration
Students keep repeating or rehearsing the definition	6	37
Students generate their own examples of the new words used in a sentence	4	21

Source: Powell, G. (1980, December). *A meta-analysis of the effects of "imposed" and "induced" imagery upon word recall.* Paper presented at the annual meeting of the National Reading Conference, San Diego, CA. (ERIC Document Reproduction Service No. Ed 199 644)

4. Direct vocabulary instruction works. Probably the most straightforward research finding relative to vocabulary is that direct instruction enhances achievement. In a major review of the research on vocabulary, researchers Stahl and Fairbanks (1986) found that teaching general vocabulary directly had an overall effect size of .32. While this is not a huge effect size, it has practical significance. It means that teaching vocabulary directly increases student comprehension of new material by 12 percentile points. To illustrate, assume that two students of equal ability are asked to read and understand new information. Student A, however, is in a program where about 10 to 12 new vocabulary words are taught each week. According to Nagy and Herman (1984), this is the typical number of words provided to students in vocabulary programs. Student B does not receive this instruction. Now assume that Students A and B take a test on the new content and that

Student B receives a score that places him at the 50th percentile relative to other students in the class. All else being equal, Student A will receive a score that places her at the 62nd percentile on that same test simply because she received systematic vocabulary instruction.

5. Direct instruction on words that are critical to new content produces the most powerful learning. The effects of vocabulary instruction are even more powerful when the words selected are those that students most likely will encounter when they learn new content. Specifically, the research by Stahl and Fairbanks (1986) indicates that student achievement will increase by 33 percentile points when vocabulary instruction focuses on specific words that are important to what students are learning. To illustrate, again consider Students A and B, who have been asked to read and understand new content. Student B, who has not received systematic vocabulary instruction, receives a score on the test that puts her at the 50th percentile. Student A, who has received systematic instruction on words *that have been specifically selected because they are important to the new content,* will obtain a score that puts him at the 83rd percentile.

Classroom Practice in Vocabulary Terms and Phrases

Identifying Critical Terms and Phrases

Given the effect of direct vocabulary instruction on student achievement, one obvious instructional activity is to identify terms and phrases that are critical to a topic and provide direct instruction on those terms and phrases. It is probably best to limit the number of critical terms and phrases for any given topic. For example, a teacher presenting a three-week unit on a specific topic might identify five key terms and phrases related to that topic. The following example shows this selection in the context of teaching students a novel.

> Mrs. Locke had always provided a list of vocabulary terms for each of the chapters in the novels she was teaching in her high school literature class. In the past, she gave 20–25 words in advance of each chapter. She noticed that the students treated the words almost like a spelling list—writing definitions, but not trying to learn or use the terms and phrases. She also found that sometimes she had to "stretch" to find that many words in each chapter.
>
> When Mrs. Locke changed her strategy, she gave students only about 5–7 words for each chapter. Sometimes the words were not taken directly from the chapter, but were selected because they would help students understand the context of the novel. For example, when she taught Ray Bradbury's *Fahrenheit 451*, she gave the students words like censorship, dystopian fiction, dual imagery, and nemesis. Learning these words provided students with a basis for understanding some of the more complex and abstract aspects of the novel.

A Process for Teaching New Terms and Phrases

Probably the most powerful way to teach new terms and phrases is to use an instructional sequence that allows for multiple exposures to students in multiple ways. The following five-step process can be a powerful tool for teaching new terms and phrases.

> *Step 1.* Present students with a brief explanation or description of the new term or phrase.
>
> *Step 2.* Present students with a nonlinguistic representation of the new term or phrase.
>
> *Step 3.* Ask students to generate their own explanations or descriptions of the term or phrase.
>
> *Step 4.* Ask students to create their own nonlinguistic representation of the term or phrase.

Step 5. Periodically ask students to review the accuracy of their explanations and representations.

The following example shows the use of this process in a high school literature unit.

Step 1. Present students with a brief explanation or description of the new term or phrase. A few days after the class had started reading the novel *Fahrenheit 451,* Mrs. Locke introduced a new word by telling one student that he should not read the book that was sitting on his desk. Naturally, the student looked surprised. She went on to say that he should read only those books approved by her. She walked over to another student and remarked that she noticed that he was keeping a journal and that it should be turned in at the end of the class to be "checked" in case the student had written anything incriminating. Finally, she told the students that they should always check with her before buying any new CDs so that she could approve their choices. The students looked at one another wondering what was going on. After a long silence, Mrs. Locke asked the students to describe what she was doing. Ben said, "You were taking charge of our thinking." Joanne thought that she was being unfair. One student stated that the teacher had no right to tell them what to read, write about, or listen to. Mrs. Locke explained to the students that they had just experienced a dramatization of the word *censorship.*

Step 2. Present students with a nonlinguistic representation of the new term or phrase. Mrs. Locke then drew a sketch on the board that depicted her dramatization of the word. The picture, she explained, shows a flame engulfing a book, a person speaking, a symbol of religion, and a newspaper.

Step 3. Ask students to generate their own explanations or descriptions of the term or phrase. Mrs. Locke asked the students to work in pairs to generate their own descriptions or explanations for the term *censorship.* Renatta wrote, "Censorship is wrong. It is taking away a person's right to think for himself."

Step 4. Ask students to create their own nonlinguistic representation of the term or phrase. The students also generated their own nonlinguistic representations. Most students used webbing techniques to represent the word, but some used sketches. One student drew a sketch of himself with bandannas around his eyes, his mouth, his ears, and his wrists to show that censorship was like a gag put on all of his senses.

Step 5. Periodically ask students to review the accuracy of their explanations and representations. For the next two weeks, as the students read the novel, they reviewed their definitions and sketches for the term *censorship,* adding new insights.

Research and Theory on Details

Details, another specific type of knowledge, are highly specific pieces of information. They include facts, time sequences, cause/effect sequences, and episodes. Figure 11.3 further explains these types of details.

We have found two generalizations that teachers can use to guide instruction in details:

1. Students should have systematic, multiple exposures to details. Perhaps the

FIGURE 11.3

Details

Facts

Facts are a specific type of informational content. Facts convey information about specific persons, places, living and nonliving things, and events. They commonly articulate information such as the following:

- The characteristics of a specific person (e.g., Thomas Jefferson served as president of the United States from 1801 to 1809).
- The characteristics of a specific place (e.g., Paris is in the country of France).
- The characteristics of specific living and nonliving things (e.g., my dog, Tuffy, is a golden retriever; the Empire State Building is more than 100 stories high).
- The characteristics of a specific event (e.g., construction began on the Leaning Tower of Pisa in 1174).

Time Sequences

Time sequences include important events that occurred between two points in time. For example, the events that occurred between President Kennedy's assassination on November 22, 1963, and his burial on November 25, 1963, are organized as a time sequence in most people's memories. First, one thing happened, then another, then another.

Cause/Effect Sequences

Cause/effect sequences involve events that produce a product or an effect. A causal sequence can be as simple as a single cause for a single effect. For example, the fact that the game was lost because a certain player dropped the ball in the end zone can be organized as a causal sequence. More commonly, however, effects have complex networks of causes; one event affects another that combines with a third event to affect a fourth that then affects another, and so on. For example, the events leading up to the U.S. Civil War can be organized as a casual sequence.

Episodes

Episodes are specific events that have

- A setting (e.g., a particular time and place).
- Specific participants.
- A particular duration.
- A specific sequence of events.
- A particular cause and effect.

For example, the events of the Watergate burglary and its effects on the Nixon presidency can be organized as an episode: The episode occurred at a particular time and place; it had specific participants; it lasted for a specific duration of time; it involved a specific sequence of events; it was caused by specific events; and it had a specific effect on the United States.

---

most striking findings in the research on details is that students must encounter details rather frequently if they are to learn facts, dates, and other details at a deep enough level to understand and recall them. Specifically, research by Nuthall (1999; Nuthall & Alton-Lee, 1995) indicates that students should be exposed to details at least three or four times before anyone can legitimately expect them to remember those details or use them in any meaningful way. In addition, researchers have found that, in general, the time between exposures to details should not exceed about two days. This interval, created by the need for multiple exposures to details and the need for those exposures to be relatively close in time, has been called the "time window" for learning (Rovee-Collier, 1995).

To illustrate, assume that the topic of the Battle of Gettysburg has been introduced to students in a section of a textbook. The teacher and the students read the section aloud and discuss it. Within two days, this same topic must be revisited in some way. The teacher can simply engage students in a discussion of the content, or he might present more information in the form of a brief presentation, have students read another section in the textbook, show a film, and so on. Within another two days, the information must be revisited again, and then again within two days after that.

2.   **Details are highly amenable to "dramatic" instruction.** Another interesting finding regarding the teaching of details is that different types of instruction produce different effects on student learning. Specifically, student understanding and recollec-tion of detail is different depending on whether instruction is verbal, visual, or dramatic. Figure 11.4 describes the differ-ing effects on learning of these types of instruction.

As its name implies, *verbal* instruction involves telling students about details or having them read about details. Although verbal instruction has fairly impressive ef-fects on students' understanding and recall of details immediately after instruction and a year later, it has the weakest effect of the three. *Visual* instruction emphasizes some form of nonlinguistic representation. We saw in Chapter 6 that this might involve graphic representations, pictures and pic-tographs, or creating mental pictures or concrete representations. The effects on learning for this technique are better than verbal instruction both immediately after instruction and one year later. Its effects are not as strong, however, as the effect for the third category of instruction—*dramatiza-tion*. When instruction emphasizes dramati-zation, students either observe a dramatic

---

FIGURE 11.4

Types of Instruction and Effect on Learning

Instruction	Effect Size (ES) Immediately After Instruction	ES After 12 Months
Verbal Instruction	.74	.64
Visual Instruction	.90	.74
Dramatic Instruction	1.12	.80

Source: Data computed from Nuthall, 1999, and Nuthall & Alton-Lee, 1995.

enactment of the details or are involved in a dramatic enactment of the details. As Figure 11.4 illustrates, this type of instruction has the strongest effects both immediately after instruction and one year later.

Classroom Practice in Details

Multiple Exposures

During a unit of instruction, teachers expose students to many, many details: facts, time sequences, episodes, and so on. Certainly students cannot process *all* of this information at a deep enough level to remember and use it at a later date. Consequently, a sound instructional strategy is to plan a unit in such a way that key details are identified—details that students are expected to know in depth. In addition, teachers should find ways to expose students to these details multiple times—at least three—and that, ideally, these exposures are no more than two days apart. The following example shows how a middle school teacher provided multiple exposures during a unit on mythology.

Ms. Sanders' class at Dry Creek Middle School is beginning a unit on Greek and Roman Mythology. Before starting, Ms. Sanders identifies the details that are critical to the unit and then considers ways to expose the class to these details several different times. She decides that she wants the class to know about significant gods and

goddesses and what they represent. Also she wants students to understand certain key myths and the ways gods, goddesses, and humans interact in the myths.

On the first day of the unit, Ms. Sanders reads a myth aloud and engages the class in a discussion in which she introduces significant gods and goddesses by their Greek and Roman names, talks about their attributes, and shows the class a picture of each—from classical art. The next day the class watches a film about early Greek architecture that contains numerous examples of gods and goddesses and depictions of their lives on the walls of early Greek buildings. For homework, Ms. Sanders assigns readings about the Trojan War.

Later that week, Ms. Sanders divides the class into small groups of two to three students. She assigns each group a particular god or goddess and asks them to design a hat symbolizing that god or goddess's attributes. Students present their hat to the class and explain its meaning.

Dramatic Representation of Key Details

Given that dramatic representation of key details has a significant effect on student learning, teachers should plan instruction to ensure that it occurs. Elementary schoolteachers probably use drama more often than do secondary teachers, but we need to remember that *all* learners can benefit from this technique. The following example describes a high school science classroom in which students were involved in a dramatic enactment:

Ms. Schlieman's sophomores had just finished reading about the circulatory system.

She knew that, for many students, this was the second or third time they had studied this system but was amazed at the limited understanding and retention of information her students exhibited. She decided to use a technique she knew would work—acting out the process. She asked the students to form several groups: One group was to be the blood; each of the other groups was to be an organ of the body. Each of the organ groups had to create a tunnel through which the blood group would flow. Students had to act out what happens to the organ and the blood as it moves through the organ. Some organs take things from the blood, others add things to it; sometimes blood changes its color. When the groups were ready, the blood group "flowed" around the room from organ to organ. Mrs. Schlieman periodically stopped the action (especially when the giggling was out of control) and discussed with all groups what was going on at that point. The class, at the students' request, repeated this enactment several times, adding more details each time.

Research and Theory on Organizing Ideas

Organizing ideas, such as generalizations and principles, are the most general type of declarative knowledge.[1] The statement, "Specific battles sometimes disproportionately influence the outcome of a war," is a generalization. Although vocabulary terms and details are important, generalizations

[1] *Note:* We have not included *concepts* as organizing ideas because, technically defined, they are synonymous with generalizations (see Gagne, 1977).

help students develop a broad knowledge base because they transfer more readily to different situations.

For instance, the preceding generalization about battles applies to wars generally—across countries, situations, and ages, whereas a fact about the Battle of Gettysburg is a specific event that does not directly transfer to other situations. This is not to say that details are unimportant. On the contrary, to truly understand generalizations, students must be able to support them with exemplifying facts. For instance, to understand the generalization about the influences of specific battles, students need a rich set of illustrative facts, one of which is probably that regarding the Battle of Gettysburg. Figure 11.5 explains generalizations and principles in more detail.

The following generalizations can serve to guide instruction in organizing ideas:

1. **Initially, students commonly have misconceptions about organizing ideas.** A great deal of research has demonstrated that students frequently have misconceptions about generalizations and principles when they are first introduced to them. In addition, it is not easy to change these misconceptions (Gilbert, Osborne, & Fensham, 1982; Hewson & Hewson, 1983; Spiro, Coulson, Feltovich, & Anderson, 1994). One meta-analytic study conducted by Guzzetti and others (1993) compared the effectiveness of various instructional techniques relative to correcting misconcep-

---

FIGURE 11.5

Organizing Ideas

Generalizations

Generalizations are statements for which examples can be provided. For example, the statement, "U.S. presidents often come from families that have great wealth or influence," is a generalization for which one can provide examples. It is easy to confuse some generalizations with some facts.

Facts identify characteristics of specific persons, places, living and nonliving things, and events, whereas generalizations identify characteristics about classes or categories of persons, places, living and nonliving things, and events. For example, the statement, "My dog, Tuffy, is a golden retriever," is a fact. The statement, "Golden retrievers are good hunters," however, is a generalization. In addition, generalizations identify characteristics about abstractions. Specifically, information about abstractions is always stated in the form of generalizations. The following are examples of the various types of generalizations:

◆ *Characteristics of classes of persons* (e.g., It takes at least two years of training to become a fireman).
◆ *Characteristics of classes of places* (e.g., Large cities have high crime rates).
◆ *Characteristics of classes of living and nonliving things* (e.g., Golden retrievers are good hunting dogs; Firearms are the subject of great debate).
◆ *Characteristics of classes of events* (e.g., The Super Bowl is the premiere sporting event each year).
◆ *Characteristics of abstractions* (e.g., Love is one of the most powerful human emotions).

Principles

Principles are specific types of generalizations that deal with relationships. In general, there are two types of principles found in school-related declarative knowledge: *cause/effect principles* and *correlational principles*.

◆ *Cause/effect principles*—Cause/effect principles articulate causal relationships. For example, the sentence, "Tuberculosis is caused by the tubercle bacillus" is a cause/effect principle. Although not stated here, understanding a cause/effect principle includes knowledge of the specific elements within the cause/effect system and the exact relationships those elements have to one another. That is, to understand the cause/effect principle regarding tuberculosis and the bacterium, one would have to understand the sequence of events that occur, the elements involved, and the type and strength of relationships between those elements. In short, understanding a cause/effect principle involves a great deal of information.

◆ *Correlational principles*—Correlational principles describe relationships that are not necessarily causal in nature, but in which a change in one factor is associated with a change in another factor. For example, the following is a correlational principle: "The increase in lung cancer among women is directly proportional to the increase in the number of women who smoke." Again, to understand this principle, a student would have to know the specific details about this relationship. Specifically, a student would have to know the general pattern of this relationship, that is, the number of women who have lung cancer changes at the same rate as the number of women who smoke cigarettes.

These two types of principles are sometimes confused with cause/effect sequences. A cause/effect sequence applies to a specific situation, whereas a principle applies to many situations. The causes of the Civil War taken together represent a cause/effect sequence. They apply to the Civil War only. The cause/effect principle linking tuberculosis and the tubercle bacillus, however, can be applied to many different situations and many different people. Physicians use this principle to make judgments about many situations and people. The key distinction between principles and cause/effect sequences is that principles can be exemplified in a number of situations, whereas cause/effect sequences cannot—they apply to a single situation only).

FIGURE 11.6

Strategies for Correcting Misconceptions

Strategy	No. of Effect Sizes (ESs)	Ave. ES	Percentile Gain
Activate prior knowledge	14	.08	3
Discussion	11	.51	19
Argumentation	3	.80	79

tions. Figure 11.6 lists these strategies and their effect sizes.

As Figure 11.6 shows, simply activating prior knowledge—asking students to *recall* what they know about a specific organizing idea—produces very little conceptual change. Having students *discuss* what they know about an organizing idea produces significantly more conceptual change probably because it facilitates the infusion of new perspectives and ideas generated by discussion. The biggest conceptual change comes when students must provide a sound defense or *argument* for their position, or are presented with a sound argument or a sound defense relative to an organizing idea.

2. **Students should be provided opportunities to apply organizing ideas.** Ross (1988) conducted an extensive review of studies relating to organizing ideas. Of the many findings in that review, one of the most useful to the classroom teacher is that students learn the most when teachers ask students to *apply* generalizations and principles once they understand them. This im-

plies that more instructional time and energy should be focused on having students use organizing ideas than initially understanding them. Of course, it is important to design instruction so that students first understand generalizations and principles. But once students initially grasp these ideas, students should apply them frequently and in a variety of situations.

Classroom Practice in Organizing Ideas

Making Sure That Students Can Clearly Articulate Statements of Generalizations and Principles and Provide Numerous Examples

Generalizations and principals are complex enough that teachers should ensure that students can state them clearly and that they can offer a variety of examples, including those that the teachers presented and those they have identified for themselves. The following example shows how this process might play out in the context of a high school history lesson.

> Daniel stated, "A democratic people cannot stay in that governing state forever. At some point there has to be a change."
>
> "I'm not really following," said Jewel. "Can you state that in a different way?"
>
> "OK, how about 'Governments must change, because the governed will demand change'?"
>
> Mrs. Bamberry overheard the conversation that the group was having as part of their study of the topic "ideal state of government." She heard Daniel trying to explain to the others that democracies would eventually end up with tyrants as their leaders. Mrs. Bamberry was surprised at Daniel's depth of understanding. Daniel even quoted Plato whose ideas they had discussed the previous day: "Plato stated that the governing system would change on account of the *desire*. Democracies treat all desires as equally good, so that means that anything goes. But the desires of some inevitably get in the way of the desires of others, so a democracy will become increasingly chaotic."
>
> "Daniel, can you back that up?" she asked. "Can you give us some examples of democracies that have collapsed into tyrannies?"
>
> Daniel's reply was quick in coming: "The most contemporary examples include when Mussolini came to power in Italy, or Hitler in Germany. In both cases, what Plato referred to as "desire" of a tyrant, led one person to take advantage of the chaos of the democratic state (the desire of the many)."
>
> "Plato," explained Mrs. Bamberry, "described the various states, and among them the *ideal state*. The ideal state was, by the way, not a democracy."
>
> "That's right," said Daniel, "but the irony of Plato's argument was that in Greek history, the tyrannies tended to precede the democracies; he was just making an argument for the *ideal state*; that state, for Plato, was the aristocracy, by *his* own rules."

Helping Students Increase Their Understanding of Generalizations and Principles and Clear Up Misconceptions About Them

If it becomes apparent that students have misconceptions about organizing ideas, the teacher might present examples that expose the flaws in their thinking. If students' understanding seems accurate, but at a surface level only, the teacher can provide opportunities for the students to use and enhance their understanding by presenting a novel situation in which the generalization or principle would apply. The following example shows how teachers can guide students in clearing up misconceptions and deepening their knowledge.

> Michaela's 5th grade classmates came to class with many new examples of the generalization that *people tend to buy things quickly when the supply is decreasing*. Michaela raised her hand and added to the conversation, "Whenever companies notice that people want something, they make sure the supply is low so they can raise the price. People pay because they will think that there is a shortage. That's what my dad says." Other students nodded in agreement.
>
> "Wait a minute, Michaela," replied her teacher. "That might be true sometimes, but not always. What if you were selling lemon-

ade on a hot day? Would you want people to think that you didn't have very much or would you want them to know that you had plenty and they could buy two?"

The teacher explained that companies, in general, increase the supply when the demand increases. She provided the students with numerous examples and went on a Web site called "Econopolis" that provided even more examples. She also described the economics principle that supported it. Michaela, and the other students, began to understand that supply, in most cases, needs to follow demand. Their teacher was relieved.

Research and Theory on Skills

Mental skills come in two different forms: *tactics* and *algorithms* (see Snowman & McCown, 1984).

+ Tactics consist of general rules governing an overall flow of execution, rather than a set of steps that must be performed in a specific order. For example, a tactic for reading a histogram might include rules that address (1) identifying the elements depicted in the legend, (2) determining what is reported on each axis of the graph, and (3) determining the relationship between the elements on the two axes. Although there is a general pattern to these rules, there is no rigid or set order.

+ Algorithms are mental skills that have specific outcomes and steps. Performing

multicolumn subtraction is an illustration of an algorithm. Although the steps in a tactic do not have to be performed in a set order, the steps in an algorithm generally do. Obviously, changing the order in which you perform the steps of multicolumn subtraction will dramatically change the answer that you compute.

For the most part, all the generalizations described in Chapter 5 on "practice" apply directly to skill learning. Consequently, when teaching students new skills, teachers should recall the generalizations described in that section. In addition, the following generalizations may help guide instruction in skills.

1. **The discovery approach is difficult to use effectively with skills.** A common misconception in education is that "discovering" how to perform a skill or tactic is always better than being directly taught the skill or process. This misconception probably gained favor in reaction to a previously held misconception that drill and practice in specific steps are always the best way to teach skills (Anderson, J. R., Reder, & Simon, 1997). Although the discovery approach has captured the fancy of many educators, there is not much research to indicate its superiority to other methods. Indeed, some researchers have made strong assertions about the lack of effectiveness of discovery learning, particularly as it relates

to skills. For example, researchers McDaniel and Schlager (1990) note: "In our view, discovery learning does not produce better skill" (p. 153).

Some skills are not amenable to discovery learning. For example, consider the skills of addition, subtraction, multiplication, and division. To have students discover the steps involved in these computational procedures makes little sense. Although it is probably true that students would certainly understand these skills well if they were required to discover their steps, it is also true that this would take an inordinate amount of time.

Although no magic list can be provided for those algorithms and tactics that are best suited to a discovery approach, a useful rule of thumb might be that the more variation there is in the steps that can be used to effectively execute a skill, the more amenable the skill is to discovery learning. For example, if five specific steps must be followed in a specific order to properly use a piece of equipment in a science laboratory, then it is questionable whether the best approach is for students to discover these five steps and their order of execution. It might be better to demonstrate those steps and then provide opportunities for students to alter them to suit their individual needs and styles. On the other hand, a tactic that can be executed in a number of ways, like that used when reading a bar graph, is probably a good candidate for discovery learning.

2. **When teachers use discovery learning, they should organize examples into categories that represent the different approaches to the skill.** One of the best examples of an effective discovery approach with skill-based knowledge is Cognitively Guided Instruction (CGI; see Carpenter, T. P., Fennema, & Peterson, 1987; Carpenter, T. P., Fennema, Peterson, Chiang, & Loef, 1989; Fennema, Carpenter, & Franke, 1992; Fennema, Carpenter, & Peterson, 1989; Peterson, Carpenter, & Fennema, 1989; Peterson, Fennema, & Carpenter, 1989). Using this approach, teachers can encourage primary students to "design" their own strategies for solving problems. Within CGI,

> Children are not shown how to solve the problems. Instead each child solves them in any way that s/he can, sometimes in more than one way, and reports how the problem was solved to peers and teacher. The teacher and peers listen and question until they understand the problem solutions, and then the entire process is repeated. Using information from each child's reporting of problem solutions, teachers make decisions about what each child knows and how instruction should be structured to enable that child to learn (Fennema, Carpenter, & Franke, 1992, p. 5).

Key to the success of this powerful discovery-oriented approach is the teacher's awareness of the types of problems that form the basis for a more complex understanding of computational facts and problem-solving strategies. Figure 11.7 shows these problem types.

FIGURE 11.7

Types of Word Problems

Problem Type			
Join	*(Result Unknown)* Connie had 5 marbles. Juan gave her 8 more marbles. How many marbles does Connie have altogether?	*(Change Unknown)* Connie has 5 marbles. How many more marbles does she need to have 13 marbles altogether?	*(Start Unknown)* Connie had some marbles. Juan gave her 5 more marbles. Now she has 13 marbles. How many marbles did Connie have to start with?
Separate	*(Result Unknown)* Connie had 13 marbles. She gave 5 to Juan. How many marbles does Connie have left?	*(Change Unknown)* Connie had 13 marbles. She gave some to Juan. Now she has 5 marbles left. How many marbles did Connie give to Juan?	*(Start Unknown)* Connie had some marbles. She gave 5 to Juan. Now she has 8 marbles left. How many marbles did Connie have to start with?
Part-Part-Whole	*(Whole Unknown)* Connie has 5 red marbles and 8 blue marbles. How many marbles does she have?	*(Part Unknown)* Connie has 13 marbles. Five are red and the rest are blue. How many blue marbles does Connie have	
Compare	*(Difference Unknown)* Connie has 13 marbles. Juan has 5 marbles. How many more marbles does Connie have than Juan?	*(Compare Quantity Unknown)* Juan has 5 marbles. Connie has 8 more than Juan. How many marbles does Connie have?	*(Reference Unknown)* Connie has 13 marbles. She has 5 more marbles than Juan. How many marbles does Juan have?

Source: Franke, M. L., Levi, L., & Empson, S. B. (1991). *Children's mathematics: Cognitively guided instruction.* Portsmouth, NH: Heinemann. Adapted by permission.

Notice that we have organized the problems in Figure 11.7 into specific categories based on the strategies used to solve them. With this detailed system of problem types, a teacher can effectively guide student inquiry. As students practice a specific type of problem, they devise and test out strategies for that type. Categorizing problems into distinct types focuses the students' inquiry. In short, for inquiry to be effective, teachers need to place examples of the skill that is the target of the discovery approach into well-organized categories that represent different ways of executing the skill. As students work through the different categories, they develop different ways of performing the skill.

3. Skills are most useful when learned to the level of automaticity. One highly generalizable research finding relative to skill learning is that skills must be learned at a level at which they require little or no conscious thought. Technically, this is referred to as learning a skill to the level of automaticity (see Anderson, J. R., 1983; Fitts & Posner, 1967; LaBerge & Samuels, 1974). To do this, students must engage in practice that gradually becomes *distributed*, as opposed to *massed*. To illustrate, in the beginning stages of learning a skill, practice sessions will be spaced very close to one another—preferably every day. These practice sessions are *massed*. Over time, the interval between practice sessions becomes longer and longer; thus practice sessions are *distributed* over time.

Classroom Practice in Skills

Facilitating the Discovery Approach to Skills

As we mentioned in the previous section, when teachers use a discovery approach to teach a specific skill, they should organize examples to represent different types of strategies. As students progress through each category of examples, they should be asked to design strategies for that particular category of example. When students have worked through the examples, they should contrast the strategies devel-oped for the different categories. The following example illustrates this in the context of driver's education.

> The students in Mr. Prado's drivers' education class were skilled enough in their driving that he thought that they were ready to learn to drive on different surfaces. To capture their attention and interest, Mr. Prado decided to have students discover different techniques for different driving surfaces rather than teach the techniques directly. With the help of a specially designed computer program in the driving simulator, he was able to expose students to a variety of driving surfaces—dry pavement, wet pavement, oil-slicked pavement, snow-covered pavement, gravel, and a rutted dirt surface. Using the simulator, he had students drive on all six surfaces. After all students had "driven" the simulator for a particular type of surface, he asked them to discuss the techniques specific to that surface. When all students had driven on all surfaces, the students worked in small groups to identify strategies that were common to all surfaces and strategies specific to each type of surface.

Planning for Distributed Practice and Emphasizing Its Importance

When teachers design lesson plans for teaching a skill, they typically decide how much class time and how many homework assignments will be dedicated to initially practicing the skill (i.e., providing time for *massed* practice). It is not as common, however, for teachers to plan for *distributed* practice. One remedy for this common oversight is to write into a planning calendar exactly when distributed practice is going to occur. Further, when a skill is taught near the end of the year, the teacher might recommend to the students a specific summer schedule for distributed practice, explaining to them the importance of achieving automaticity and the role of distributed practice. Obviously, some students will not follow the schedule; but, at a minimum, students might increase their understanding of the process of learning a skill. The following example shows how a high school teacher became aware of the importance of distributed practice.

> Ms. Chimes was an English teacher but also taught piano lessons in the evenings and on weekends. One Saturday, she was explaining to a new piano student that the practice schedule for each student was worked out far in advance. She explained further that even when a student became quite good at a skill, there was still a need to keep going back and practicing it. As she talked to the student, something occurred to her. She applied her understanding of practice meticulously to her piano teaching, but did not follow the same regimen in her English class. This might explain why she had to do so much reteaching of the writing and research skills she taught early in the year. She felt a little foolish when she realized how long she had been using practice effectively with piano, but had not transferred it to her English classroom.

Research and Theory on Processes

Processes are similar to skills in some ways and different in other ways. They are similar in that they produce some form of product or new understanding. For example, the tactic of reading a bar graph produces a new understanding of the relationship between two variables. The process of writing produces a new composition. Processes, however, have a much higher tolerance for variation relative to the steps involved than do skills. For example, there are not a great many ways to go about reading a bar graph, but many different ways to engage in the process of writing. We might say that processes are more "robust" than skills in terms of how they can be performed.

By definition, processes are not amenable to a "step-by-step" instructional approach. But most students could still do with some guidance in the general aspects of the process. For example, it is common to provide a description of the various components involved in writing. Occasionally, teachers refer to this approach as "process writing." Consider the following phrases (or adaptations of them) that many teachers use for the writing process:

1. Prewriting
2. Writing
3. Revising

Within each of these major components of the writing process, more specific subcomponents are identified, such as the following:

3. Revising:
  • Revising for the overall logic of the composition
  • Revising for effective transitions

◆ Revising for word choice and phrasing

◆ Revising for subject-verb agreement

◆ Revising for spelling and punctuation

We have drawn two generalizations that teachers can use to guide instruction with processes:

1. **Students should practice the parts of a process in the context of the overall process.** Obviously, teachers should present students with the components and subcomponents of a process and provide practice in all of them. The research on writing offers an insight into how this is best accomplished. Specifically, Hillocks (1986) examined four approaches to teaching writing, which can be described as follows:

1. *Presentation:* The teacher explains what good writing is and gives examples.

2. *Natural process:* The teacher has students engage in a great deal of free writing, individually and in groups.

3. *Focused practice:* The teacher structures writing tasks to emphasize specific aspects of writing.

4. *Skills:* The teacher breaks down writing into its component parts and then provides practice, sometimes in isolation, on each part.

Figure 11.8 shows the effect sizes for each of these approaches.

According to Figure 11.8, the approach that produces the best learning is focused practice. In these situations, teachers present students with the components and subcomponents of the process and then structure writing tasks to emphasize a specific component or subcomponent. For example, a teacher might assign a composition that emphasizes the subcomponent of revising for overall logic or revising for transitions. Note that simply explaining to

---

FIGURE 11.8
Effect Sizes for Various Approaches to Writing

Approach	No. of Effect Sizes (ESs)	ES
Presentation	4	.02
Natural process	9	.19
Focused practice	10	.44
Skills	6	.17

students what good writing is (i.e., the "presentation" approach) resulted in the lowest effect size in the studies reviewed by Hillocks (1986). Note also how small the effect sizes were for simply having students write a great deal (i.e., the "natural process" approach) or practicing the components and subcomponents in isolation (i.e., the "skills" approach).

2. Teachers should emphasize the metacognitive control of processes. Processes, by definition, involve complex interactions of component skills. Consequently, a student must not only have mastery over the component skills, but must be able to control the interactions of these elements. This is commonly referred to as *metacognitive control* (see Scardamalia & Bereiter, 1985). In fact, in a major review of research on instruction, Wang, Haertel, and Walberg (1993) found that strategies that emphasized the metacognitive aspects of learning a process had some of the largest effect sizes of all categories considered.

The research of Michael Pressley and his associates (see Pressley, Woloshyn, & Associates, 1995; Pressley, Goodchild, Fleet, Zajchowski, & Evans, 1989) has provided some explicit guidelines for developing metacognitive control in students:

◆ Provide plenty of guided practice by having students use the strategies for as many appropriate tasks as possible, providing reinforcement and feedback on how the stu-

dents can improve their execution of the strategies.
◆ Encourage students to monitor their performance when using the strategies.
◆ Encourage generalization of the strategies by having students use them with different types of materials in the various content areas, as well as their continued use (Pressley, Woloshyn, & Associates, 1990, p. 18).

Classroom Practice in Processes

Providing a General Model of the Overall Components and Subcomponents of Processes

Students need a fair amount of guidance when first learning a complex process. One of the best ways to provide this guidance is to give them a model of the overall components and subcomponents of the process. The following is an example of using a model in the context of reading instruction in elementary school:

Students in every grade level at Buena Vista Elementary are presented with the following major components of the Reading Process.

Experience
Select Text
Identify What Is Known/Set Purpose
Construct Meaning
Use/Reflect

At every grade level, the overall process is reviewed as students learn new subcomponents for each phase. For example, to "construct meaning," students work on their ability to decode, to predict, to confirm and disconfirm predictions, to make inferences, to create mental pictures, and to clear up confusions. Teachers at Buena Vista use the reading process consistently so that by the time students leave the 5th grade, they are familiar with the interactive components of reading and have developed fluency in the individual components.

Focusing on Specific Subcomponents Within the Context of the Entire Process

As stated in the first generalization in the previous section, students really shouldn't practice the subcomponents of a complex process in isolation. Instead, they should practice the subcomponents in the context of the overall process. For example, when engaged in the overall process of reading, students might practice making and confirming predictions, as opposed to making and confirming predictions in isolation of the overall process. This level of focus requires use of metacognitive skills (see the second generalization). The following activities are useful in helping students focus on specific subcomponents of a process.

◆ Help students to articulate clearly the specific subcomponent (e.g., skill, strategy) that they are going to practice and to set criteria for evaluating their own progress

◆ Provide a variety of assignments over time that require students to use the targeted skill or strategy within the context of the process.

◆ Encourage students to self-assess but also provide feedback on the targeted skill or strategy. To help students focus, avoid giving feedback on other aspects of the process.

The following example describes how teachers might help students engage in focused practice within the context of the research process.

As the middle and high school teachers finished their model of the research process they would present to students, they were struck with the sheer number of skills and strategies students would be asked to use. In the ensuing discussion, the high school teachers admitted that they had often wondered, aloud, if middle school teachers actually taught the research process. It seemed that every year, when students were asked to do research, they had to be guided through the entire process as if they were hearing it for the first time. It was now more obvious why this happened. Students were never asked to focus on and master any specific skill within the research process.

The teachers set a goal for their next work session. They decided to identify the specific skills and strategies within the overall research process that would be the focus for each year. They also began to design a feedback sheet that teachers would use across grade levels. The sheet contained the components of the research process and the extensive list of subcomponent skills and strategies. For each grade level, the feedback sheet highlighted the subcomponents that would be the focus for that year. For example, a subcomponent for focus in 7th grade was accessing information from the Internet and evaluating the quality of the source. For the 10th grade, it was developing a thesis statement and narrowing the topic. By designing this feedback sheet, the teachers hoped they would begin to see real progress in students' skills at the research process.

◆ ◆ ◆

In this chapter, we have considered specific strategies for teaching five types of knowledge: vocabulary terms and phrases, details, organizing ideas, skills and tactics, and processes. Planning instruction at this level of detail makes teaching more precise, and learning more efficient.

12

USING THE NINE CATEGORIES IN INSTRUCTIONAL PLANNING

If teachers are familiar with the research and practice presented in Chapters 2 through 11, this knowledge will likely influence the way they plan for instruction. As a refresher, here's a list of the nine categories of strategies that have a strong effect on student achievement:

+ Identifying similarities and differences.
+ Summarizing and note taking.
+ Reinforcing effort and providing recognition.
+ Homework and practice.
+ Nonlinguistic representations.
+ Cooperative learning.
+ Setting objectives and providing feedback.
+ Generating and testing hypotheses.
+ Questions, cues, and advance organizers.

To plan with the intent of systematically using the strategies presented in this book, teachers might think about unit planning as involving the following three phases:

+ At the *beginning* of a unit, include strategies for setting learning goals.
+ *During* a unit, include strategies
  – for monitoring progress toward learning goals.
  – for introducing new knowledge.
  – for practicing, reviewing, and applying knowledge.
+ At the *end* of a unit, include strategies for helping students determine how well they have achieved their goals.

In this chapter, we have provided an extended example of unit planning following this model in the context of a hypothetical unit on weather.

◆ ◆ ◆

At the Beginning of a Unit of Instruction

Ms. Becker, a 6th grade teacher, was teaching a unit on weather. When she planned the unit, she first considered strategies focused on identifying and communicating goals. Figure 12.1 shows the strategies she considered.

Near the beginning of the unit, Ms. Becker clearly articulated the learning goals for students. She constructed these goals by consulting her district's curriculum, examining her textbook, and considering what she knew about the interests of 6th graders. Deciding to include interdisciplinary content, she identified four goals for science, one for geography, and one for language arts.

Ms. Becker gave a copy of the learning goals to each student, using "I" statements to help students relate at a more personal level (see Figure 12.2). After students read through the goals, Ms. Becker provided a brief description of each.

Ms. Becker also asked students to identify personal learning goals. Students first examined the learning goals she had presented, but then identified more specific goals that interested them. She also encouraged students to set goals for becoming better learners. To illustrate these two types

---

FIGURE 12.1
Instructional Strategies for Use at the *Beginning* of a Unit

Setting Learning Goals

1. Identify clear learning goals. (See Chapter 8)
2. Allow students to identify and record their own learning goals. (See Chapter 8)

---

of goals, Ms. Becker provided the following examples:

My personal learning goals:

1. Personal Learning Goal 1: I will try to understand what the deal is with El Niño. How it influences weather where I live. Everyone talks about it, but I don't get it.

2. Personal Learning Goal 2: I will learn more about the kinds of destruction tornadoes create. I think it is different from what you see after a hurricane. I loved the movie *Twister* and I have been interested in tornadoes ever since.

After providing time for the students to write their personal goals in their "learning journals," Ms. Becker asked them to pair up and to do the following:

◆ Share their goals with one another.
◆ Brainstorm ways to achieve their goals.

When Ms. Becker began planning this unit, she took the time to consider potential

---

FIGURE 12.2

Example of Unit Goals: The Power of the Weather

As a result of this unit, I will:

Unit Learning Goal 1: Science
I will . . . Understand key weather terms, including:

air mass	atmosphere	hurricane
front (cold, warm, stationary)	evaporation	tornado
precipitation	El Nino	cirrus, cumulus, stratus
barometer	humidity	air pressure

Unit Learning Goal 2: Science
I will . . . Understand how interactions of air masses, as they move across the oceans and land, create fronts and how these fronts become thunderstorms, tornadoes, and hurricanes.

Unit Learning Goal 3: Science
I will . . . Know the major types of clouds, how they are formed, and to what weather patterns they are related.

Unit Learning Goal 4: Science
I will . . . Be able to use a barometer and a thermometer to gather, analyze, and interpret weather data.

Unit Learning Goal 5: Geography
I will . . . Understand how physical geographic factors—weather—influence human behavior and historic events.

Unit Learning Goal 6: Language Arts
I will . . . Understand elements of literature, specifically how weather, as part of setting, influences plot.

Personal Learning Goals: During this unit, I will . . .

_____

_____

_____

_____

_____

---

student attitudes that might get in the way of the students' setting and achieving their learning goals. She knew that, in the past, 6th graders had not been highly interested in the subject of weather. In fact, she assumed that they considered the topic mundane. To make the unit more personally meaningful to students, she decided to build on the theme of how weather influences people's lives—their own lives, historical events, and even people's lives in fiction. To launch the unit with this theme in the forefront, she gave the following assignment:

1. Try to remember an event in your life that was influenced by weather. Make some notes about what happened and how you and others were influenced. Be ready to share your stories.

2. Interview several people—parents, grandparents, friends—and ask them to tell you about a time they can remember when their lives were influenced by weather. For example, I had a friend once who met a man when she was stranded at an airport because of a storm. That man later became her husband. Be ready to share stories that illustrate interesting, although not too personal, examples of how weather influenced the lives of people you know.

During a Unit

During the unit, Ms. Becker employed techniques that related to three areas: monitoring learning goals; introducing new knowledge; and practicing, reviewing, and applying knowledge.

Monitoring Learning Goals

Figure 12.3 lists the strategies Ms. Becker considered to help students monitor progress toward learning goals.

As the weather unit progressed, Ms. Becker helped students monitor their

---

FIGURE 12.3

Instructional Strategies to Use *During* a Unit

Monitoring Learning Goals

1. Provide students feedback and help them self-assess their progress toward achieving their goals. (See Chapter 8)

2. Ask students to keep track of their achievement of the learning goals and of the effort they are expending to achieve the goals. (See Chapter 4)

3. Periodically celebrate legitimate progress toward learning goals. (See Chapter 4)

---

progress. Further, she asked them to monitor the effort they were putting into the unit assignments. Her 6th grade team had always asked students to keep a spiral notebook entitled "My Learning"; but for this unit, Ms. Becker had them set up the pages using a format that would help them track their progress. Periodically throughout the unit, students were asked to focus on specific unit learning goals and their personal goals. Then, after reflecting on their experiences, they were to self-assess, on a four-point scale, how well they were achieving their goals and again, on a four-point scale, how much effort they were expending. Finally, they were to identify and briefly describe behaviors that had worked well for them, as well as those behaviors they needed to change to be more successful.

To help students self-assess each goal and to assess their effort, Ms. Becker reviewed with them some general rubrics that would provide the consistent criteria for their evaluation. When she handed out the rubrics, she left space on the page after each rubric level for students to make their own notes and personalize the rubrics. The students knew that these rubrics, with their personal notes added, would be handed in at the end of the unit along with their learning journals. Students were either provided class time to write in their learning journals or were asked to write in their journals as part of their homework. Ms. Becker regularly set aside a few minutes at the beginning or end of class for students to share some of their journal entries in small-group discussions. She encouraged students to use their groups to help each other clear up confusions, to make suggestions for improving performance, and to congratulate each other when significant progress was made.

Introducing New Knowledge

In planning, Ms. Becker made a distinction between those things she would do to introduce knowledge to students and those things she would do to help students practice, review, and apply knowledge. Figure 12.4 shows some of the strategies she considered to introduce knowledge.

Ms. Becker used activities that relied on cooperative learning groups, as well as individual activities. Before she introduced each major topic, she gave the cooperative groups a few minutes to talk about what

---

FIGURE 12.4

Instructional Strategies for Use *During* a Unit

Introducing New Knowledge

1. Guide students in identifying and articulating what they already know about the topics (Chapter 10).

2. Provide students with ways of thinking about the topic in advance (Chapter 10).

3. Ask students to compare the new knowledge with what is known (Chapter 2).

4. Have students keep notes on the knowledge addressed in the unit (Chapter 3).

5. Help students represent the knowledge in nonlinguistic ways, periodically sharing these representations with others (Chapter 6).

6. Ask students to work sometimes individually, but other times in cooperative groups (Chapter 7).

---

they already knew—or *thought* they knew—about the topic and what they thought they would probably be learning. The recorder for the group jotted down ideas from each group member and kept the list in her notebook.

After the individual learning time for each topic, groups reconvened and compared what they learned with what they thought they knew. Ms. Becker listened to groups before and after the lessons, both to modify upcoming lessons based on what students already knew and to evaluate what students had learned.

As the teacher introduced each new topic—whether by watching a film, reading the text, or engaging in class discussion—she

FIGURE 12.5

Sample Student Notebook

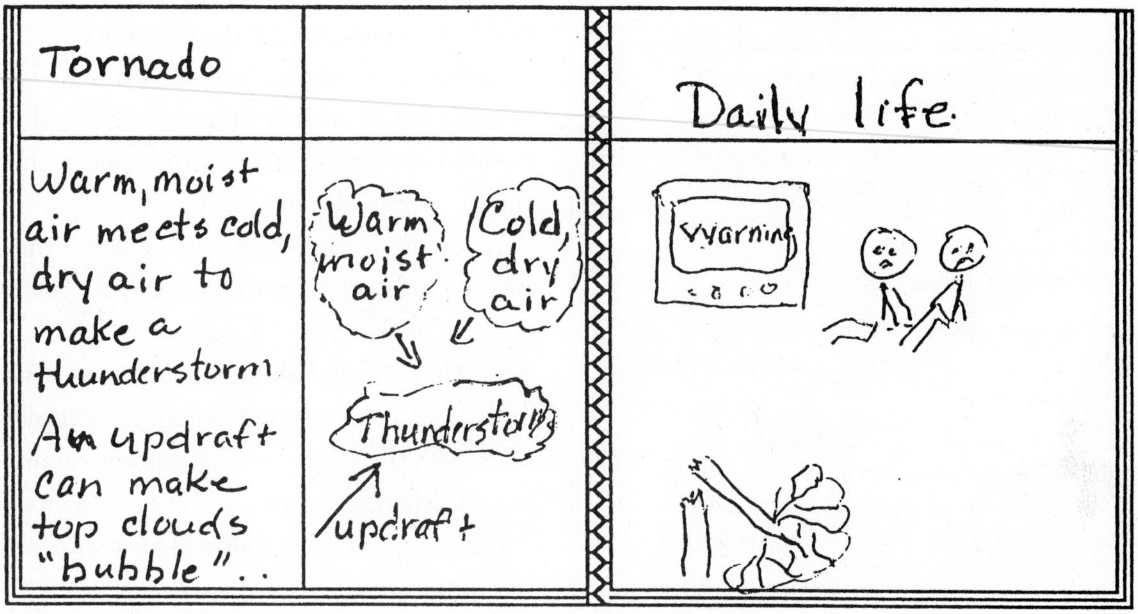

asked students to open their notebooks and set up the pages as shown in Figure 12.5.

On the left-hand page, students took notes, using the note-taking format that Ms. Becker had taught them (see also Figure 3.15 and the discussion of note-taking in Chapter 3). This format included both written notes and graphic representations. On the right-hand page, students described or drew pictures of some possible effects of the weather phenomenon that was explained on the left. This helped students keep focused on the theme of the unit—weather influencing people's lives. They could make up possible effects (like "A picnic is ruined") or could write or depict actual and fictional events with which they were familiar.

Practicing, Reviewing, and Applying Knowledge

Figure 12.6 lists instructional strategies that Ms. Becker considered to help students practice, review, and apply their knowledge.

As the unit progressed, Ms. Becker assigned different types of homework, depending on the type of knowledge she was introducing. The following are two examples of homework she designed for review and practice:

◆ *After vocabulary terms were introduced,* students' homework was to add the term to their unit vocabulary list by using what they learned in class, their own experiences, and several Web sites Ms. Becker provided. For each term, students were to describe the

---

FIGURE 12.6

Instructional Strategies for Use *During* Unit

Practicing, Reviewing,
and Applying Knowledge

1. Assign homework that requires students to practice, review, and apply what they have learned; however, be sure to give students explicit feedback on the accuracy of all homework (Chapter 5).

2. Engage students in long-term projects that involve generating and testing hypotheses (Chapter 9).

3. Ask students to revise the linguistic and nonlinguistic representations of knowledge in their notebooks as they refine their understanding of the knowledge (Chapters 3 and 6).

---

term in their own words, create a graphic representation or draw a picture of the word, and list other words that are related to it. (Students typically used approximately half a page for each vocabulary term. They kept these vocabulary pages together in a section of their notebooks.)

♦ *After the skill of reading a barometer was introduced,* Ms. Becker provided students with worksheets containing pictures of five types of barometers that students were to read. During the evening, students read each set of barometers and recorded their readings. The next day, students paired up and shared their readings. Ms. Becker then presented them with the correct readings. Students again discussed the accuracy of their readings with particular attention to problems they had.

The day after a homework assignment, Ms. Becker asked students to place their homework on their desks. She reviewed each student's homework as they worked independently or in groups. On a removable sticky note, she simply wrote a number 1–4 to indicate the degree of accuracy or depth of understanding the students had demonstrated in their homework. She also pointed out any major misconceptions they might have. If she did not get to each student's work during class, she collected the pages and handed them back the next day.

Ms. Becker wanted students to use what they learned about weather patterns and about how weather influences people's lives. She, therefore, considered several options for long-term projects that students could complete. The following list shows her initial ideas:

1. Investigation of a hypothetical past event. What if the weather had been different on the day of a historical event—either a famous event or an event from your or someone else's past? Describe the sequence of weather-related events that led up to the event. Then describe a different sequence and explain how history might have been different if the weather had been different. Do the same for a fictional event.

2. Decision Making. We have read and heard accounts of some of the major storms of the 20th century. If scientists had to select which storm was *the* storm of the century, which do you think it would be? Set up a decision-making matrix to select which storm you think should win this distinction. Use criteria that reflect both your understanding of the impact of weather on people's lives and your understanding of weather elements that characterize storms.

Once you have selected what *you* believe to be the "Storm of the Century," we will visit a Web site that depicts what scientists decided and compare your decision with the storm that actually was selected by scientists.

3. System Analysis. Select one major weather event and describe how each element of the event influenced the other elements (such as, the temperature influenced the moisture in the air, which influenced, etc.) Then, change one element and describe how the other elements would be affected. Next, go back and change a different element, and describe what would happen to the other elements.

After considering these three possible projects, Ms. Becker selected one and de-

veloped it into the project described in Figure 12.7.

At the End of a Unit

Ms. Becker thought carefully about how to bring the unit to completion in a way that enhanced the learning for every student in her class. Figure 12.8 lists some of the strategies she considered.

Ms. Becker had always been committed to providing students with useful feedback. She was meticulous about providing stu-

---

FIGURE 12.7

Sample Long-Term Project

What if...

We are going to use your technical understanding of weather and what you know about history to create a new job—a "histo-meteorologist."

Select one of the examples—that you found or that was presented in class—of a historical event that would have been different with different weather. Compose a short oral or written description of that event as if you were a historian and a meteorologist all in one (a "histo-meteorologist"). Describe the event as if you have a special report each night on the nightly news. Be sure to use technical terms accurately.

You might, for example, describe the day the *Titanic* sailed as "a beautiful clear day, high pressure dominated, and there wasn't a cumulus, cirrus, or stratus cloud in the sky. But then a few cirrus clouds began to appear and a warm air mass moved in and met up with a cold front, forcing water vapor to. . . ." You might then end with "The captain of the *Titanic* was heard to say that if it hadn't been for that low-lying stratus

cloud, we might have hit that iceberg. That would have been a real tragedy."

You might instead be a literary-meteorologist and do the same thing for an event in a story. Change the weather and describe it using scientific terms. Then explain what would have happened differently to the plot by changing the weather. (Idea: *What if* . . . Cinderella had run into a major thunderstorm and never made it to the ball?)

You get the idea.

This task requires investigation of a hypothetical past event. You must take what you understand about weather cause-effect patterns and apply it to a specific situation that you get to make up. You will be assessed on the following elements:

♦ How well you use your skills of investigation to describe a hypothetical past event.

♦ How well you use your understanding of causes of weather.

FIGURE 12.8

Instructional Strategies for Use at the *End* of a Unit

Helping Students Determine How Well They Have Achieved Their Goals

1. Provide students with clear assessments of their progress on each learning goal (Chapters 4 and 8).

2. Have students assess themselves on each learning goal and compare these assessments with those of the teacher (Chapters 4 and 8).

3. Ask students to articulate what they have learned about the content and about themselves as learners (Chapters 4 and 8).

---

dents with immediate feedback on their assignments, both in writing and orally during class. When a unit or long-term assignment was completed, she always tried to schedule one-on-one conferences with students, but it was difficult to do this very often and very well. Whenever she provided extensive written feedback on long-term assignments, she noticed that many of the students simply looked at the grade and did not read her comments. Given her commitment to feedback, she had recently applied for and had just received a small grant to purchase class sets of audiotape recorders, each with a set of earphones. Now she had a new approach to giving feedback.

Learning Logs

First, Ms. Becker asked all the students to identify a final page in their learning log,

on which they were to evaluate the extent to which they had achieved each unit goal and each personal goal. The format they used included a column for the student's final assessment for each goal, and the teacher's final assessment of each goal. It also included space for students to comment on each goal and to make final comments about what they learned about weather and about themselves as learners. Students handed in this learning log as part of their portfolio from the unit.

Audiotape Assessments

As Ms. Becker reviewed each portfolio and evaluated the students on their achievement of the goals, she communicated her feedback through brief written statements and rubric scores *and by recording more detailed feedback on audiotape.* Because she was doing less writing, she was able to finish grading the unit more quickly than usual and yet provide more extensive comments.

On the day Ms. Becker returned the portfolios, she handed each student the audiotape and a tape player with earphones. She gave them time to listen to her comments with the portfolio in front of them. Although every student did not listen with the same level of concentration, she noticed that as they listened, many students were flipping through their portfolio and examining parts of assignments as they listened to her critique on the tape.

♦ ♦ ♦

Benefits of Strategic Planning

The research-based instructional strategies considered before, during, and after the unit greatly influenced Ms. Becker's planning. In some cases, planning with the strategies in mind validated what she had always done. But it also helped her to re-think some of her classroom practices. Explicitly planning a unit with an eye toward employing specific strategies *before*, *during*, and *after* a unit, raised the quality of her planning and teaching. More important, it enhanced student achievement.

13

AFTERWORD

In the first chapter of this book, we began with a "call to arms," so to speak. We asserted that the field of education is at a turning point in its history—a point at which schooling and teaching are beginning to become more of a science than an art. Accomplishing this transformation will require at least three major efforts.

First, the research on instruction and schooling must be synthesized and made readily available to educators. This book is intended as a small but important step to make research understandable and useful. No doubt other similar resources will soon be available to educators.

Second, schools and school districts must provide high-quality staff development relative to effective practices identified by the research. That is, simply presenting teachers with instructional techniques that are backed by the research is insufficient to effect change. Indeed, research has

consistently shown that changing the practice of schooling requires far more than simply presenting educators with new strategies in an "inservice workshop" (see Fullan, 1993; Guskey, 2000; Joyce & Showers, 1980). Some of the elements we believe are necessary for change to occur in day-to-day classroom practice are described here. It should come as no surprise that these elements are drawn directly from the research presented in this book:

◆ **Adequate modeling and practice.** Learning a complex skill mandates that a person properly demonstrate the skill, with attention to the many variations in implementation the skill may require. In addition, acquiring a complex skill demands extensive practice during which time one learns the skill to a level at which it can be executed with little conscious thought. We discussed these facts in depth in Chapters 5 and 12 of this book. Although many of the techniques presented in this book are certainly known to teachers, they are, nonetheless, skills that teachers must master if they are to use the skills and strategies effectively in the classroom. Schools and districts should provide teachers with training experiences that include effective modeling of strategies, along with substantial time to practice those strategies.

◆ **Feedback.** One of the primary messages in Chapter 8 of this book is that students need accurate and timely feedback as they are learning new knowledge. So, too, must schools and districts provide teachers with accurate and timely feedback relative to their acquisition of the strategies in this book. An effective and efficient way to provide feedback is to ask teachers to work in study groups as they try out new strategies gleaned from this text. Members of a group might observe each other as they implement a given strategy and then "debrief" one another on those elements of the strategy that worked well and those that did not.

◆ **Allowance for differences in implementation.** Chapter 5 of this text emphasized the need for students to "shape" new skills to be compatible with their own individual needs and styles. Schools and districts must make the same allowances for teachers learning the strategies presented in this book. There is no single way to implement an instructional strategy. Although we suggest that teachers first try out the recommended format for a given strategy, we also suggest that teachers adapt strategies to their particular needs and the particular context in which they will use them.

◆ **Celebration.** Chapter 4 of this book discussed the needs of students for recognition. Again, teachers as learners have the same needs. Therefore, we strongly suggest that schools and districts organizing staff development around this book devote a formal and systematic part of the training to celebrating not only the *success* teachers are experiencing implementing strategies in their classrooms, but also the *sheer effort* they are putting into making substantive change in their classrooms. In fact, we might go so far as to say "When in doubt, celebrate!"

Third, and perhaps most important, educators must have a desire and commitment to change. There is growing sentiment that schooling, in general, is resistant to change and that classroom teachers, in particular, are almost impervious to change. There are even those who maintain that the probability of changing classroom instructional practices through staff development efforts is so small that we should not even try (see Carpenter, W. A., 2000). We believe that this is an overly pessimistic view not only of staff development, but of the profession of teaching in general.

We agree, however, that substantive change is difficult. Busy teachers who have been doing things the same way for a fair amount of time will have many valid reasons for not trying a new strategy. What is clearly required to alter the status quo is a sincere desire to change and a firm commitment to weather the inevitable storms as change occurs. We should note that we are not so naive as to think that all teachers in a school will have the requisite level of desire and commitment. But collectively, as authors, we have had more than 50 years of experience in staff development and have come to the conclusion that a small group of educators within a school who are enthusiastic about a particular innovation can "infect" an entire staff with that enthusiasm. Quite literally, on occasion, we have seen a *single individual* in a school be the primary catalyst for substantive change.

Consequently our call to arms is not for everyone. In fact, it is intended for those only who have been sitting and waiting for such an invitation. We believe that your desire and commitment is perhaps the most powerful resource for change that exists in public education. We encourage you to nurture that desire and commitment, and we hope that this book will be a useful tool to you as you transform education from an art to a science.

The following table provides a quick reference to percentile gains or losses associated with specific effect sizes. To illustrate how to use this table, assume that a research study found that the use of a specific strategy produced an effect size of .20. You should first locate .20 in the column labeled "Effect Size." In this case, it can be found in the first column. To the immediate right of this number is the percentile gain associated with the effect size. In this case, it is 8. This means that the score of the average person in the group that *used* the instructional strategy would be 8 percentile points *higher* than the score of the average person in the group that *did not use* the instructional strategy.

Conversion Table for Effect Size/Percentile Gain

Effect Size	Percentile Gain	Effect Size	Percentile Loss
0.00	0	0.00	0
0.02	1	−0.02	−1
0.05	2	−0.05	−2
0.08	3	−0.08	−3
0.10	4	−0.10	−4
0.13	5	−0.13	−5
0.15	6	−0.15	−6
0.18	7	−0.18	−7
0.20	8	−0.20	−8
0.23	9	−0.23	−9
0.25	10	−0.25	−10
0.28	11	−0.28	−11
0.31	12	−0.31	−12
0.33	13	−0.33	−13
0.36	14	−0.36	−14
0.39	15	−0.39	−15
0.41	16	−0.41	−16
0.44	17	−0.44	−17
0.47	18	−0.47	−18
0.50	19	−0.50	−19
0.52	20	−0.52	−20
0.55	21	−0.55	−21
0.58	22	−0.58	−22
0.61	23	−0.61	−23
0.64	24	−0.64	−24
0.67	25	−0.67	−25
0.71	26	−0.71	−26
0.74	27	−0.74	−27
0.77	28	−0.77	−28
0.81	29	−0.81	−29
0.84	30	−0.84	−30
0.88	31	−0.88	−31
0.92	32	−0.92	−32
0.95	33	−0.95	−33
1.00	34	−1.00	−34
1.04	35	−1.04	35
1.08	36	−1.08	−36
1.13	37	−1.13	−37
1.18	38	−1.18	−38
1.23	39	−1.23	−39
1.28	40	−1.28	−40
1.34	41	−1.34	−41
1.41	42	−1.41	−42
1.48	43	−1.48	−43
1.56	44	−1.56	−44
1.65	45	−1.65	−45
1.75	46	−1.75	−46
1.88	47	−1.88	−47
2.05	48	−2.05	−48
2.33	49	−2.33	−49

References

Alexander, P. A. (1984). Training analogical reasoning skills in the gifted. *Roeper Review, 6*(4), 191–193.

Alexander, P. A., & Judy, J. E. (1988). The interaction of domain-specific and strategic knowledge in academic performance. *Review of Educational Research, 58*, 375–404.

Alexander, P. A., Kulikowich, J. M., & Schulze, S. K. (1994). How subject-matter knowledge affects recall and interest. *American Educational Research Journal, 31*(2), 313–337.

Alvermann, D. E., & Boothby, P. R. (1986). Children's transfer of graphic organizer instruction. *Reading Psychology, 7*(2), 87–100.

Anderson, J. R. (1983). *The architecture of cognition.* Cambridge, MA: Harvard University Press.

Anderson, J. R. (1990). *Cognitive psychology and its implications* (3rd ed.). New York: Freeman.

Anderson, J. R. (1995). *Learning and memory: An integrated approach.* New York: Wiley.

Anderson, J. R., Reder, L. M., & Simon, H. A. (1997). *Applications and misapplications of cognitive psychology to mathematics education.* Unpublished manuscript, Carnegie Mellon University, Pittsburgh, PA.

Anderson, L., Evertson, C., & Brophy, J. (1979). An experimental study of effective teaching in first-grade reading groups. *Elementary School Journal, 79*, 193–223.

Anderson, T.H., & Armbruster, B.B. (1986). *The value of taking notes during lectures.* (Tech. Rep. No. 374). Cambridge, MA: Bolt, Beranek & Newman; and Urbana, IL: Center for the Study of Reading. (ERIC Document Reproduction Service No. ED 277 996)

Anderson, V., & Hidi, S. (1988/1989). Teaching students to summarize. *Educational Leadership, 46*, 26–28.

Armbruster, B. B., Anderson, T. H., & Meyer, J. L. (1992). Improving content-area reading using instructional graphics. *Reading Research Quarterly, 26*(4), 393–416.

Armbruster, B. B., Anderson, T. H., & Ostertag, J. (1987). Does text structure/summarization instruction facilitate learning from expository text? *Reading Research Quarterly, 22*(3), 331–346.

Armbruster, B. B., Anderson, T. H., & Ostertag, J. (1987). Does text structure/summarization instruction facilitate learning from expository text. *Reading Research Quarterly, 22*(3), 331–346.

Athappilly, K., Smidchens, V., & Kofel, J. W. (1983). A computer-based meta-analysis of the effects of modern mathematics in comparison with traditional mathematics. *Educational Evaluation and Policy Analysis, 5*(4), 485–493.

Aubusson, P., Foswill, S., Barr, R., & Perkovic, L. (1997). What happens when students do simulation-role-play in science. *Research in Science Education, 27*(4), 565–579.

Ausubel, D. P. (1968). *Educational psychology: A cognitive view.* New York: Holt, Rinehart & Winston.

Balli, S. J. (1998). When mom and dad help: Student reflections on parent involvement with homework. *Journal of Research and Development in Education, 31*(3), 142–148.

Balli, S. J., Demo, D. H., & Wedman, J. F. (1998). Family involvement with children's homework: An intervention in the middle grades. *Family Relations: Interdisciplinary Journal of Applied Family Studies, 47*(2), 149–157.

Balli, S. J., Wedman, J. F., & Demo, D. H. (1997). Family involvement with middle-grades homework: Effects of differential prompting. *Journal of Experimental Education, 66*(1), 31–48.

Bandura, A., & Schunk, D. H. (1981). Cultivating competence, self-efficacy, and intrinsic interest through proximal self-motivation. *Journal of Personality and Social Psychology, 41*, 568–578.

Bangert-Downs, R. L., Kulik, C. C., Kulick, J. A., & Morgan, M. (1991). The instructional effects of feedback in test-like events. *Review of Educational Research, 61*(2), 213–238.

Becker, W. C. (1977). Teaching reading and language to the disadvantaged—what we have learned from field research. *Harvard Educational Review, 47*, 518–543.

Beecher, J. (1988). *Note-taking: What do we know about the benefits: ERIC Digest #37.* Bloomington, IN: ERIC Clearinghouse on Reading, English, and Communications. (ERIC Document Reproduction Service No. EDO CS 88 12)

Bloom, B. S. (1976). *Human characteristics and school learning.* New York: McGraw-Hill.

Bond, G. W., & Smith, G. J. (1966). Homework in the elementary school. *The National Elementary School Principal, 45*(3), 46–50.

Bretzing, B. H., & Kulhary, R.W. (1979, April). Notetaking and depth of processing. *Contemporary Educational Psychology, 4*(2), 145–153.

Brewer, W. F., & Treyens, J. C. (1981). Role of schemata in memory for places. *Cognitive Psychology, 13*, 207–230.

Brophy, J. (1981). Teacher praise: A functional analysis. *Review of Educational Research, 51*, 5–32.

Brophy, J., & Good, T. (1986). Teacher behavior and student achievement. In M. Wittrock (Ed.), *Handbook of research on teaching* (pp. 328–375). New York: Macmillan.

Brown, A. L., Campione, J. C., & Day, J. (1981). Learning to learn: On training students to learn from texts. *Educational Researcher, 10*, 14–24.

Cameron, J., & Pierce, W. D. (1994). Reinforcement, reward, and intrinsic motivation: A meta-analysis. *Review of Educational Research, 64*(3), 363–423.

Carpenter, T. P., Fennema, E., & Peterson, P. L. (1987). Cognitively guided instruction: The application of cognitive and instructional science to mathematics curriculum development. In I. Wirszup & R. Streit (Eds.), *Developments in school mathematics education around the world* (pp. 397–417). Reston, VA: National Council of Teachers of Mathematics.

Carpenter, T. P., Fennema, E., Peterson, P. L., Chiang, C. P., & Loef, M. (1989). Using knowledge of children's mathematics thinking in classroom teaching: An experimental study. *American Educational Research Journal, 26*(4), 499–531.

Carpenter, W. A. (2000). Ten years of silver bullets: Dissenting thoughts on educational reform. *Phi Delta Kappan, 81*(5), 383–389.

Carrier, C. A., & Titus, A. (1981, Winter). Effects of notetaking pretraining and test mode expectations on learning from lectures. *American Educational Research Journal, 18*(4), 385–397.

Carter, J. F., & Van Matre, N. H. (1975). Note taking versus note having. *Journal of Educational Psychology, 67*(6), 900–904.

Chall, J. S. (1958). *Readability: An appraisal of research and application.* Columbus, OH: Bureau of Educational Research, Ohio State University.

Chen, Z. (1996). Children's analogical problem solving: The effects of superficial, structural, and procedural similarities. *Journal of Experimental Child Psychology, 62*(3), 410–431.

Chen, Z. (1999). Schema induction in children's analogical problem solving. *Journal of Educational Psychology, 91*(4), 703–715.

Chen, Z., Yanowitz, K. L., & Daehler, M. W. (1996). Constraints on accessing abstract source information: Instantiation of principles facilitates children's analogical transfer. *Journal of Educational Psychology 87*(3), 445–454.

Chi, M. T. H., Feltovich, P. J., & Glaser, R. (1981). Categorization and representation of physics problems by experts and novices. *Cognitive Science, 5*, 121–152.

Clement, J., Lockhead, J., & Mink, G. (1979). Translation difficulties in learning mathematics. *American Mathematical Monthly, 88*, 3–7.

Cohen, J. (1988). *Statistical power analysis for the behavioral sciences* (2nd ed.). Hillsdale, NJ: Erlbaum.

Cole, J. C., & McLeod, J. S. (1999). Children's writing ability. The impact of the pictorial stimulus. *Psychology in the Schools, 36*(4) 359–370.

Coleman, J. S., Campbell, E., Hobson, C., McPartland, J., Mood, A., Weinfeld, F., & York, R. (1966). *Equality of educational opportunity.* Washington, DC: U.S. Government Printing Office.

Cooper, H. (1989a). *Homework.* White Plains, NY: Longman.

Cooper, H. (1989b). Synthesis of research on homework. *Educational Leadership, 47*(3), 85–91.

Cooper, H., Lindsay, J. J., Nye, B., & Greathouse, S. (1998). Relationships among attitudes about homework, amount of homework assigned and completed, and student achievement. *Journal of Educational Psychology, 90*(1), 70–83.

Cooper, H., Valentine, J. C., Nye, B. & Lindsay, J. J. (1999). Relationship between five after-school activities and academic achievement. *Journal of Educational Psychology, 91*(2), 369–378.

Cooperative Learning Center. (2000). *The Cooperative Learning Center at the University of Minnesota.* [Online] Available: http://www.clcrc.com/index.html#essays.

Countryman, L. L., & Schroeder, M. (1996). When students lead parent-teacher conferences. *Educational Leadership, 53*(7), 64–68.

Covington, M. V. (1983). Motivation cognitions. In S. G. Paris, G. M. Olson, & H. W. Stevenson (Eds.), *Learning and motivation in the classroom* (pp. 139–164). Hillsdale, NJ: Lawrence Erlbaum.

Covington, M. V. (1985). Strategic thinking and the fear of failure. In J. W. Segal, S. F. Chipman, & R. Glaser (Eds.), *Thinking and learning skills: Vol. 1, Relating instruction to research* (pp. 389–416). Hillsdale, NJ: Lawrence Erlbaum.

Craske, M. L. (1985). Improving persistence through observational learning and attribution retraining. *British Journal of Educational Psychology, 55*, 138–147.

Crismore, A. (Ed.). (1985). *Landscapes: A state-of-the-art assessment of reading comprehension research: 1974–1984. Final report.* Washington, DC: U.S. Department of Education (ED 261–350).

Crooks, T. J. (1988). The impact of classroom evaluation practices on students. *Review of Educational Research, 58*(4), 438–481.

Dagher, Z. R. (1995). Does the use of analogies contribute to conceptual change? *Science and Education, 78*(6), 601–614.

Darch, C. B., Carnine, D. W., & Kameenui, E. J. (1986). The role of graphic organizers and social structure in content area instruction. *Journal of Reading Behavior, 18*(4), 275–295.

Davis, F. B. (1944). Fundamental factors of comprehension in reading. *Psychometrika, 9*, 185–197.

Davis, O. L., & Tinsley, D. (1967). Cognitive objectives revealed by classroom questions asked by social studies teachers and their pupils. *Peabody Journal of Education, 44*, 21–26.

Davis, R. B. (1984). *Learning mathematics: The cognitive science approach to mathematics education.* Norwood, NJ: Ablex.

Deci, E. L. (1971). Effects of externally mediated rewards on intrinsic motivation. *Journal of*

Personality and Social Psychology, 22, 113–120.

Deely, J. (1982). *Semiotics: Its history and doctrine.* Bloomington: Indiana University Press.

Denner, P. R. (1986). *Comparison of the effects of episodic organizers and traditional notetaking on story recall* (Final Report). Boise: Idaho State University. (ERIC Document Reproduction No. ED 270 731)

Druyan, S. (1997). Effects of the kinesthetic conflict on promoting scientific reasoning. *Journal of Research in Science Teaching, 34*(10), 1083–1099.

Duncker, K. (1945). On problem-solving (L. S. Lees, Trans.). *Psychological Monographs, 58,* 270.

Eco, U. (1976). *A theory of semiotics.* Bloomington: Indiana University Press.

Eco, U. (1979). *The role of the reader.* Bloomington: Indiana University Press.

Eco, U. (1984). *Semiotics and the philosophy of language.* Bloomington: Indiana University Press.

Einstein, G. O., Morris, J., & Smith, S. (1985, October). Notetaking, individual differences, and memory for lecture information. *Journal of Educational Psychology, 77*(5), 522–532.

El-Nemr, M. A. (1980). Meta-analysis of outcomes of teaching biology as inquiry. *Dissertation Abstracts International, 40,* 5813A.

English, L. D. (1997). Children's reasoning in classifying and solving computational word problems. In L. D. English (Ed.), *Mathematical reasoning: Analogies, metaphors and images* (pp. 191–220). Mahwah, NJ: Lawrence Erlbaum.

Evertson, C., Anderson, C., Anderson, L., & Brophy, J. (1980). Relationships between classroom behaviors and student outcomes in junior high mathematics and English classes. *American Educational Research Journal, 17,* 43–60.

Fennema, E., Carpenter, T. P., & Franke, M. L. (1992, Spring). Cognitively guided instruction. *NCRMSE Research Review, 1*(2), 5–9, 12.

Fennema, E., Carpenter, T. P., & Peterson, P. L. (1989). Teachers' decision making and cognitively guided instruction: A new paradigm for curriculum development. In F. Ellerton & M. A. (Ken) Clements (Eds.), *School mathematics: The challenge to change* (pp. 174–187). Geelong, Victoria, Australia: Deakin University Press.

Fillippone, M. (1998). *Questioning at the elementary level.* Master's thesis, Kean University. (ERIC Document Reproduction Service No. ED 417 431)

Fitts, P. M., & Posner, M. I. (1967). *Human performance.* Belmont, CA: Brooks Cole.

Flanders, N. (1970). *Analyzing teacher behavior.* Reading, MA: Addison-Wesley.

Fletcher, J. (1990). *Effectiveness and cost of interactive video disc instruction in defense training and education.* Alexandria, VA: Institute for Defense Analysis. (IDA paper No. P 2372)

Flick, L. (1992). Where concepts meet percepts. Stimulating analogical thought in children. *Science and Education, 75*(2), 215–230.

Fowler, T. W. (1975, March). *An investigation of the teacher behavior of wait-time during an inquiry science lesson.* Paper presented at the annual meeting of the National Association for Research in Science Teaching, Los Angeles. (ERIC Document Reproduction Service No. ED 108 872)

Foyle, H. C. (1985). The effects of preparation and practice homework on student achievement in tenth-grade American history (Doctoral dissertation, Kansas State University, 1984). *Dissertation Abstracts International, 45,* 2474A.

Foyle, H. C., & Bailey, G. D. (1988). Homework experiments in social studies: Implications for teaching. *Social Education, 52*(4), 292–296.

Foyle, H., Lyman, L., Tompkins, L., Perne, S., & Foyle, D. (1990). *Homework and cooperative learning: A classroom field experiment* (Tech. Report). Emporia, KS: Emporia State University. (ERIC Document Reproduction Service No. ED 350 285)

Franke, M. L., Levi, L., & Empson, S. B. (1991). *Children's mathematics: Cognitively guided instruction.* Portsmouth, NH: Heinemann.

Fraser, B. J., Walberg, H. J., Welch, W. W., & Hattie, J. A. (1987). Synthesis of educational productivity research. *Journal of Educational Research, 11*(2), 145–252.

Fullan, M. G. (1993). *Change forces: Probing the depths of educational reform.* Bristol, PA: Falmer.

Gagne, R. M. (1977). *The conditions of learning* (3rd ed.). New York: Holt, Rinehart, & Winston.

Ganske, L. (1981). Note-taking: A significant and integral part of learning environments. *Education Communication and Technology Journal (ECTJ), 29*(3), 155–175.

Gentner, D., & Markman, A. B. (1994). Structural alignment in comparison: No difference without similarity. *Psychological Science, 5*(3), 152–158.

Gerlic, I., & Jausovec, N. (1999). Multimedia: Differences in cognitive processes observed with EEG. *Educational Technology Research and Development, 47*(3), 5–14.

Gholson, B., Smither, D., Buhrman, A., & Duncan, M. K. (1997). The source of children's reasoning errors during analogical problem solving. *Applied Cognitive Psychology, 10* (Special Issue).

Gick, M. L., & Holyoak, K. J. (1980). Analogical problem solving. *Cognitive Psychology, 12,* 306–355.

Gilbert, J. K., Osborne, R. J., & Fensham, P. J. (1982). Children's science and its consequences for teaching. *Science Education, 66,* 623–633.

Glynn, S. M., & Takahashi, T. (1998). Learning from analogy—enhanced science text. *Journal of Research in Science Teaching, 35*(10), 1129–1149.

Good, T. L., Grouws, D. A., & Ebmeier, H. (1983). *Active mathematics teaching.* New York: Longman.

Gorges, T. C., & Elliott, S. N. (1995). Homework: Parent and student involvement and their effects on academic performance. *Canadian Journal of School Psychology, 11*(1), 18–31.

Gottfried, G. M. (1998). Using metaphors as modifiers: Children's production of metaphoric compounds. *Journal of Child Language, 24*(3), 567–601.

Graue, M. E., Weinstein, T., & Walberg, H. J. (1983). School-based home instruction and

learning: A quantitative synthesis. *Journal of Educational Research, 76,* 351–360.

Griffin, C., Simmons, D. C., & Kameenui, E. J. (1992). Investigating the effectiveness of graphic organizer instruction on the comprehension and recall of science content by students with learning disabilities. *Journal of Reading, Writing & Learning Disabilities International, 7*(4), 355–376.

Guskey, T. R. (2000). *Evaluating professional development.* Thousand Oaks, CA: Corwin Press.

Guszak, F. J. (1967). Teacher questioning and reading. *The Reading Teacher, 21,* 227–234.

Guzzetti, B. J., Snyder, T. E., & Glass, G. V. (1993). Promoting conceptual change in science: A comparative meta-analysis of instructional interventions from reading education and science education. *Reading Research Quarterly, 28*(2), 117–155.

Hall, L. E. (1989). The effects of cooperative learning on achievement: A meta-analysis. *Dissertation Abstracts International, 50,* 343A.

Haller, E. P., Child, D. A., & Walberg, H. J. (1988). Can comprehension be taught? A quantitative synthesis of "metacognitive studies." *Educational Researcher, 17*(9), 5–8.

Hamaker, C. (1986). The effects of adjunct questions on prose learning. *Review of Educational Research, 56,* 212–242.

Hansell, T. S. (1988). One student's learning cycle in an interpretive reading discussion. *Reading Psychology, 7*(4), 297–304.

Harrison, C. (1980). *Readability in the classroom.* Cambridge, England: Cambridge University Press.

Harter, S. (1980). The perceived competence scale for children. *Child Development, 51,* 218–235.

Hattie, J. A. (1992). Measuring the effects of schooling. *Australian Journal of Education, 36*(1), 5–13.

Hattie, J., Biggs, J., & Purdie, N. (1996). Effects of learning skills interventions on student learning: A meta-analysis. *Review of Educational Research, 66*(2), 99–136.

Hayes, J. R. (1981). *The complete problem solver.* Philadelphia, PA: The Franklin Institute.

Healy, J. M. (1990). *Endangered minds: Why our children don't think.* New York: Simon & Schuster.

Hedges, L. V. (1987). How hard is hard science, how soft is soft science? The empirical cumulativeness of research. *American Psychologist, 42*(2), 443–455.

Heller, J. I., & Reif, F. (1984). Prescribing effective human problem solving processes: Problem descriptions in physics. *Cognition and Instruction, 1*(2), 177–216.

Henk, W. A., & Stahl, N. A. (1985). *A meta-analysis of the effect of notetaking on learning from lecture.* Paper presented at the 34th Annual Meeting of the National Reading Conference. (ED 258 533)

Hewson, M. G., & Hewson, P. W. (1983). Effect of instruction using students' prior knowledge and conceptual change strategies on science learning. *Journal of Research in Science Teaching, 20,* 731–743. (Study I. D. #29)

Hidi, S., & Anderson, V. (1987). Providing written summaries: Task demands, cognitive operations, and implications for instruction. *Reviewing Educational Research, 56,* 473–493.

Hillocks, G. (1986). *Research on written composition.* Urbana, IL: ERIC Clearinghouse on Reading and Communication Skills and National Conference on Research in English.

Holland, J. H., Holyoak, K. F., Nisbett, R. E., & Thagard, P. R. (1986). *Induction: Processes of inference, learning, and discovery.* Cambridge, MA: MIT Press.

Honea, J. M., Jr. (1982, December). Wait-time as an instructional variable: An influence on teacher and student. *Clearing House, 56*(4), 167–170.

Horton, S. V., Lovitt, T. C., & Bergerud, D. (1990). The effectiveness of graphic organizers for three classifications of secondary students in content area classes. *Journal of Learning Disabilities, 23*(1), 12–22.

Hunter, J. E., & Schmidt, F. L. (1990). *Methods of meta-analysis: Correcting error and bias in research findings.* Newbury Park, CA: Sage.

Hyerle, D. (1996). *Visual tools for constructing knowledge.* Alexandria, VA: Association for Supervision and Curriculum Development.

Jencks, C., Smith, M. S., Ackland, H., Bane, J. J., Cohen, D., Grintlis, H., Heynes, B., & Michelson, S. (1972). *Inequality: A reassessment of the effects of family and schools in America.* New York: Basic Books.

Jenkins, J. R., Stein, M. L., & Wysocki, K. (1984). Learning vocabulary through reading. *American Educational Research Journal, 21*(4), 767–787.

Johnson, D. W., & Johnson, R. T. (1999). *Learning together and alone: Cooperative, competitive, and individualistic learning.* Boston: Allyn & Bacon.

Johnson, D., Maruyama, G., Johnson, R., Nelson, D., and Skon, L. (1981). Effects of cooperative, competitive, and individualistic goal structures on achievement: A meta-analysis. *Psychological Bulletin, 89*(1), 47–62.

Johnson-Laird, P. N. (1983). *Mental models.* Cambridge, MA: Harvard University Press.

Joyce, B., & Showers, B. (1980). Improving inservice training: The messages of research. *Educational Leadership, 37*(5), 379–385.

Kagan, S. (1994). *Cooperative learning.* California: Author.

Kahle, A. L., & Kelly, M. L. (1994). Children's homework problems: A comparison of goal setting and parent training. *Behavior Therapy, 25*(2), 275–290.

Keith, T. Z. (1982). Time spent on homework and high school grades: A large-sample path analysis. *Journal of Educational Psychology, 74*(2), 248–253.

Kintsch, W. (1979). On modeling comprehension. *Educational psychologist, 1,* 3–14.

Koedinger, K. R., & Anderson, J. R. (1993). Reifying implicit planning in geometry: Guidelines for model-based intelligent tutoring systems. In S. Lajoie & S. Derry (Eds.), *Computers as cognitive tools.* Hillsdale, NJ: Lawrence Erlbaum.

Koedinger, K. R., & Tabachneck, H. J. M. (1994, April). *Two strategies are better than one: Multiple strategies used in word problem solving.* Paper presented at the annual meeting of the American Educational Research Association, New Orleans.

Kohn, A. (1993). Why incentive plans cannot work. *Harvard Business Review, 71*(5), 54–63.

Kulik, C. L. C., & Kulik, J. A. (1982). Effects of ability grouping on secondary school students: A meta-analysis of evaluation findings. *American Educational Research Journal, 19*(3), 415–428.

Kulik, J. A., & Kulik, C. L. C. (1987). Effects of ability grouping on student achievement. *Equity and Excellence, 23*, 22–30.

Kulik, J. A., & Kulik, C. L. C. (1991). *Research on ability grouping: Historical and contemporary perspectives.* Storrs: University of Connecticut, National Research Center on the Gifted and Talented. (ERIC Document Reproduction Service No. ED 350 777)

Kumar, D. D. (1991). A meta-analysis of the relationship between science instruction and student engagement. *Education Review, 43*(1), 49–66.

LaBerge, D., & Samuels, S. J. (1974). Toward a theory of automatic information processing in reading. In H. Singer & R. B. Riddell (Eds.), *Theoretical models and processes of reading* (pp. 548–579). Newark, DE: International Reading Association.

Lavoie, D. R. (1999). Effects of emphasizing hypothetico-predictive reasoning within the science learning cycle on high school students' process skills and conceptual understanding in biology. *Journal of Research in Science Teaching, 36*(10), 1127–1147.

Lavoie, D. R., & Good, R. (1988). The nature and use of prediction skills in biological computer simulation. *Journal of Research in Science Teaching, 25*, 334–360.

Lawson, A. E. (1988). A better way to teach biology. *The American Biology Teacher, 50*, 266–278.

Lee, A. Y. (n.d.). *Analogical reasoning: A new look at an old problem.* Boulder: University of Colorado, Institute of Cognitive Science.

Leone, C. M., & Richards, M. H. (1989). Classwork and homework in early adolescence: The ecology of achievement. *Journal of Youth and Adolescence, 18*(6), 531–548.

Lepper, M. R. (1983). Extrinsic reward and intrinsic motivation: Implications for the classroom. In J. M. Levine & M. C. Wang (Eds.), *Teacher and student perceptions: Implications for learning* (pp. 281–318). Hillsdale, NJ: Lawrence Erlbaum.

Lepper, M. R., Greene, D., & Nisbett, R. E. (1973). Undermining children's intrinsic interest with extrinsic reward: A test of the overjustification hypothesis. *Journal of Personality and Social Psychology, 28*, 129–137.

Lin, H. (1996). The effectiveness of teaching science with pictorial analogies. *Research in Science Education, 26*(4), 495–511.

Lindsley, O. R. (1972). From Skinner to precision teaching. In J. B. Jordan & L. S. Robbins (Eds.), *Let's try doing something else kind of thing.* Arlington, VA: Council for Exceptional Children.

Lipsey, M. W., & Wilson, D. B. (1993). The efficacy of psychological, educational, and behavioral treatment. *American Psychologist, 48*(12), 1181–1209.

Lott, G. W. (1983). The effect of inquiry teaching and advanced organizers upon student outcomes in science education. *Journal of Research in Science Teaching, 20*(5), 437–451.

Lou, Y., Abrami, P. C., Spence, J. C., Paulsen, C., Chambers, B., & d'Apollonio, S. (1996). Within-class grouping: A meta-analysis. *Review of Educational Research, 66*(4), 423–458.

Lysakowski, R. S., & Walberg, H. J. (1981). Classroom reinforcement in relation to learning: A quantitative analysis. *Journal of Educational Research, 75*, 69–77.

Lysakowski, R. S., & Walberg, H. J. (1982). Instructional effects of cues, participation, and corrective feedback: A quantitative synthesis. *American Educational Research Journal, 19*(4), 559–578.

Macklin, M. C. (1997). Preschoolers' learning of brand names for visual cues. *Journal of Consumer Research, 23*(3), 251–261.

Madaus, G. F., & Stufflebeam, D. (Eds.). (1989). *Educational evaluation: Classic works of Ralph W. Tyler.* Boston: Kluwer Academic Press.

Mager, R. (1962). *Preparing instructional objectives.* Palo Alto, CA: Fearon Publishers.

Markman, A. B., & Gentner, D. (1993a). Splitting the differences: A structural alignment view of similarity. *Journal of Memory and Learning, 32,* 517–535.

Markman, A. B., & Gentner, D. (1993b). Structural alignment during similarity comparisons. *Cognitive Psychology, 25,* 431–467.

Martorella, P. H. (1991). Knowledge and concept development in social studies. In J. P. Shaver (Ed.), *Handbook of research on social studies teaching and learning* (pp. 370–399). New York: McMillan.

Marzano, R. J. (1998). *A theory-based meta-analysis of research on instruction.* Aurora, CO: Mid-continent Research for Education and Learning. (ERIC Document Reproduction Service No. ED 427 087)

Marzano, R. J., Gnadt, J., & Jesse, D. M. (1990). *The effects of three types of linguistic encoding strategies on the processing of information presented in lecture format.* Unpublished manuscript. Denver: University of Colorado at Denver.

Mason, L. (1994). Cognitive and metacognitive aspects in conceptual change by analogy. *Instructional Science 22* (3), 157–187.

Mason, L. (1995). Analogy, meta-conceptual awareness and conceptual change: A classroom study. *Educational Studies, 20*(2), 267–291.

Mason, L., & Sorzio, P. (1996). Analogical reasoning in restructuring scientific knowledge. *European Journal of Psychology of Education, 11*(1), 3–23.

Mathematical Science Education Board. (1990). *Reshaping School Mathematics.* Washington DC: National Academy Press.

Mayer, R. E. (1979). Can advance organizers influence meaningful learning? *Review of Educational Research, 49,* 371–383.

Mayer, R. E. (1989). Models of understanding. *Review of Educational Research, 59*(1), 43–64.

McDaniel, M. A., & Schlager, M. S. (1990). Discovery learning and transfer of problem-solving skills. *Cognition and Instruction, 7*(2), 129–159.

McKeown, M. G., & Curtis, M. E. (Eds.). (1987). *The nature of vocabulary acquisition.* Hillsdale, NJ: Lawrence Erlbaum.

McLaughlin, E. M. (1991, March). Effects of graphic organizers and levels of text difficulty on less-proficient fifth-grade reader's comprehension of expository text. *Dissertation Abstracts International,* Vol. 51 (9–A), 3028.

Medawar, P. B. (1967). Two conceptions of science. In J. P. Medawar (Ed.), *The art of the soluble* (pp. 114–160). London: Methuen.

Medin, D., Goldstone, R. L., & Markman, A. B. (1995). Comparison and choice: Relations between similarity processes and decision processes. *Psychonomic Bulletin & Review, 2*(1), 1–19.

Merrett, F., & Thorpe, S. (1996). How important is the praise element in the pause, prompt, and praise tutoring procedures for older, low-progress readers? *Educational Psychology, 16*(2), 193–206.

Meyer, B. J. F. (1975). *The organization of prose and its effects on memory.* Amsterdam: North-Holland Press.

Meyer, B. J. F., & Freedle, R. O. (1984). Effects of discourse type on recall. *Americans Educational Research Journal, 21*(1), 121–143.

Miller, D. L., & Kelley, M. L. (1991). Interventions for improving homework performance: A critical review. *School Psychology Quarterly, 6*(3), 174–185.

Miller, D., & Kelley, M. L. (1994). The use of goal setting and contingency contracting for improving children's homework performance. *Journal of Applied Behavioral Analysis, 27*(1), 73–84.

Morgan, M. (1984). Reward-induced decrements and increments in intrinsic motivation. *Review of Educational Research, 54*(1), 5–30.

Morgan, M. (1985). Self-monitoring of attained subgoals in private study. *Journal of Educational Psychology, 77*(6), 623–630.

Morine-Dershimer, G. (1982). Pupil perceptions of teacher praise. *Elementary School Journal, 82,* 421–434.

Muehlherr, A., & Siermann, M. (1996). Which train might pass the tunnel first? Testing a learning context suitable for children. *Psychological Reports, 79*(2), 627–633.

Mueller, D. D. (1973). Teacher questioning practices in reading. *Reading World, 12*(2), 136–145.

Nagy, W. E., & Anderson, R. (1984). The number of words in printed school English. *Reading Research Quarterly, 19*, 304–330.

Nagy, W. E., & Herman, P. A. (1984). *Limitations of vocabulary instruction* (Tech. Rep. No. 326). Urbana, IL: University of Illinois, Center for the Study of Reading. (ERIC Document Reproduction Service No. ED 248 498)

Nagy, W. E., & Herman, P. A. (1987). Breadth and depth of vocabulary knowledge: Implications for acquisition and instruction. In M. C. McKeown & M. E. Curtis (Eds.), *The nature of vocabulary instruction* (pp. 19–36). Hillsdale, NJ: Erlbaum.

Nagy, W. E., & Herman, P. A. (1987). Learning words from context during normal reading. *American Educational Research Journal, 24*(2), 2437–270.

Nash, R. J., & Shiman, D. A. (1974). The English teacher as questioner. *English Journal, 63*, 42–45.

National Research Council (1996). *National science education standards*. Washington, DC: National Academy Press.

Newby, T. J., Ertmer, P. A., & Stepich, D. A. (1995). Instructional analogies and the learning of concepts. *Educational Technology Research and Development, 43*(1), 5–18.

Newell, A. & Rosenbloom, P. S. (1981). Mechanisms of skill acquisition and the law of practice. In J. R. Anderson (Ed.), *Cognitive skills and their acquisition*. Hillsdale, NJ: Erlbaum

Newton, D. P. (1995). Pictorial support for discourse comprehension. *British Journal of Educational Psychology, 64*(2), 221–229.

Nuthall, G. (1999). The way students learn. Acquiring knowledge from an integrated science and social studies unit. *Elementary School Journal, 99*(4), 303–341.

Nuthall, G. & Alton-Lee, A. (1995). Assessing classroom learning. How students use their knowledge and experience to answer classroom achievement test questions in science and social studies. *American Educational Research Journal, 32*(1), 185–223.

Nye, P., Crooks, T. J., Powlie, M., & Tripp, G. (1984). Student note-taking related to university examination performances. *Higher Education, 13*(1), 85–97.

Oakes, J. (1985). *Keeping track: How schools structure inequality*. New Haven, CT: Yale University Press.

Osman, M., & Hannafin, M. J. (1994). Effects of advance organizing questioning and prior knowledge on science learning. *Journal of Educational Research, 88*(1), 5–13.

Paivio, A. (1969). Mental imagery in associative learning and memory. *Psychological Review, 76*, 241–263.

Paivio, A. (1971). *Imagery and verbal processing*. New York: Holt, Rinehart & Winston.

Paivio, A. (1990). *Mental representations: A dual coding approach*. New York: Oxford University Press.

Palincsar, A. S., & Brown, A. L. (1984). Reciprocal teaching of comprehension fostering and comprehension monitoring activities. *Cognition and Instruction, 1*(2), 117–175.

Palincsar, A. S., & Brown, A. L. (1985). Reciprocal teaching: Activities to promote reading with your mind. In T. L. Harris & E. J. Cooper (Eds.), *Reading, thinking and concept development: Strategies for the classroom*. New York: The College Board.

Paschal, R. A., Weinstein, T., & Walberg, H. J. (1984). The effects of homework on learning: A quantitative synthesis. *Journal of Educational Research, 78*, 97–104.

Pennsylvania Department of Education. (1973). *Study on homework: Homework policies in the public schools of Pennsylvania and selected states in the nation*. Harrisburg, PA: Author.

Percy, W. (1975). *The message in the bottle*. New York: Farrar, Strauss & Giroux.

Perkins, P. G., & Milgram, R. B. (1996). Parental involvement in homework: A double-edge sword. *International Journal of Adolescence and Youth, 6*(3), 195–203.

Peterson, P. L., Carpenter, T. P., & Fennema, E. (1989). Teachers' knowledge of students' knowledge in mathematics problem solving: Correlational and case analyses. *Journal of Educational Psychology, 81*(4), 558–569.

Peterson, P. L., Fennema, E., & Carpenter, T. P. (1989). Teachers' knowledge of students' mathematics problem solving knowledge. In J. Brophy (Ed.), *Advances in research on teaching: Teachers subject matter knowledge* (Vol. II, pp. 195–221). Greenwich, CT: JAI Press.

Pflaum, S. W., Walberg, H. J., Karegianes, M. L., & Rasher, S. P. (1980). Reading instruction: A quantitative analysis. *Educational Researcher, 9*(7), 12–18.

Powell, G. (1980, December). *A meta-analysis of the effects of "imposed" and "induced" imagery upon word recall.* Paper presented at the annual meeting of the National Reading Conference, San Diego, CA. (ERIC Document Reproduction Service No. Ed 199 644)

Pressley, M., Goodchild, F., Fleet, J., Zajchowski, R., & Evans, E. D. (1989). The challenges of classroom strategy instruction. *Elementary School Journal, 89,* 301–342.

Pressley, M., Symons, S., McDaniel, M., Snyder, B. L., & Turnure, J. E. (1988). Elaborative interrogation facilitates acquisition of confusing facts. *Journal of Educational Psychology, 80,* 268–278.

Pressley, M., Tenenbaum, R., McDaniel, M., & Wood, E. (1990). What happens when university students try to answer prequestions that accompany textbook material? *Contemporary Educational Psychology, 15,* 27–35.

Pressley, M., Woloshyn, V., & Associates. (1995). *Cognitive strategy instruction that really improves children's academic performance.* Cambridge, MA: Brookline Books.

Pressley, M., Wood, E., Woloshyn, V., Martin, V., King, A., & Menke, D. (1992). Encouraging mindful use of prior knowledge: Attempting to construct explanatory answers facilitates learning. *Educational Psychologist, 27*(1), 91–109.

Pruitt, N. (1993). *Using graphics in content area subjects.* Master's thesis, Kean College of New Jersey. (ERIC Document Reproduction Service No. ED 355 483)

Raphael, T. E., & Kirschner, B. M. (April, 1985). *The effects of instruction in compare/contrast text structure on sixth grade students' reading comprehension and writing production.* Paper presented at the annual meeting of the American Educational Research Association, Chicago.

Rattermann, M. J., & Gentner, D. (1998). More evidence for a relational shift in the development of analogy: Children's performance on a causal-mapping task. *Cognitive Development, 13*(4), 453–478.

Redfield, D. L., & Rousseau, E. W. (1981). A meta-analysis of experimental research on teacher questioning behavior. *Review of Educational Research, 51*(2), 237–245.

Reeves, L. M., & Weisberg, R. W. (1994). On the concrete nature of human thinking: Content and context in analogical transfer. *Educational Psychology, 13*(3–4), 245–258.

Richardson, A. (1983). Imagery: Definitions and types. In A. A. Sheikh (Ed.), *Imagery: Current theory, research, and application* (pp. 3–42). New York: John Wiley & Sons.

Ripoll, T. (1999). Why this made me think of that. *Thinking and Reasoning, 4*(1), 15–43.

Risner, G. P., & Nicholson, J. I. (1996). *The new basal readers: What levels of comprehension do they promote?* (ERIC Document Reproduction Service No. ED 403 546)

Risner, G. P., Nicholson, J. I., & Webb, B. (1994). *Levels of comprehension promoted by the Cooperative Integrated Reading and Composition (CIRC) Program.* Florence: University of North Alabama. (ERIC Document Reproduction Service No. ED 381 751)

Robinson, D. H., & Kiewra, K. A. (1996). Visual argument: Graphic organizers are superior to outlines in improving learning from text. *Journal of Educational Psychology, 87*(3), 455–467.

Roderique, T. W., Pulloway, E. A., Cumblad, C. L., Epstein, M. H. (1994). Homework: A survey of policies in the United States. *Journal of Learning Disabilities, 27*(8), 481–487.

Romberg, T. A., & Carpenter, T. P. (1986). Research on teaching and learning mathematics: Two disciplines of scientific inquiry. In M. C. Wittrock (Ed.), *Handbook of research on teaching* (3rd ed.). New York: Macmillan.

Rosenberg, M. S. (1989). The effects of daily homework assignment in the acquisition of basic skills by students with learning disabilities. *Journal of Learning Disabilities, 22*(5), 314–323.

Rosenshine, B., & Meister, C. C. (1994). Reciprocal teaching: A review of the research. *Review of Educational Research, 64*(4), 479–530.

Rosenshine, B., Meister, C., & Chapman, S. (1996). Teaching students to generate questions. A review of the intervention studies. *Review of Educational Research, 66*(2), 181–221.

Rosenthal, R. (1991). *Meta-analytic procedures for social research.* Newbury Park, CA: Sage.

Ross, B. H. (1984). Rememberings and their effects on learning a cognitive skill. *Cognitive Psychology, 16*, 371–416.

Ross, B. H. (1987). This is like that: The use of earlier problems and the separation of similarity effects. *Journal of Experimental Psychology, 13*(4), 629–639.

Ross, J. A. (1988). Controlling variables: A meta-analysis of training studies. *Review of Educational Research, 58*(4), 405–437.

Rovee-Collier, C. (1995). Time windows in cognitive development. *Developmental Psychology, 31*(2), 147–169.

Rowe, M. (1974). Wait-time and rewards as instructional variables, their influence on language, logic and fate control. Part 1 wait-time. *Journal of Research in Science Teaching, 11*, 81–94.

Sanders, W. L. &, Horn, S. P. (1994). The Tennessee value-added assessment system (TVAAS): Mixed-model methodology in educational assessment. *Journal of Personnel Evaluation in Education, 8*, 299–311.

Scardamalia & Bereiter, C. (1985). Fostering the development of self-regulation in children's knowledge processing. In S. F. Chipman, J. W. Segal, & R. Glaser (Eds.), *Thinking and learning skills: Vol. 2. Research and open questions* (pp. 563–577). Hillsdale, NJ: Lawrence Erlbaum Associates.

Scheerens, J., & Bosker, R. (1997). *The foundations of educational effectiveness.* New York: Pergamon.

Schunk, D. H. & Cox, P. D. (1986). Strategy training and attributional feedback with learning disabled students. *Journal of Educational Psychology. 73* (3), 201–209.

Seligman, M. E. P. (1990). *Learned optimism.* New York: Pocket Books.

Seligman, M. E. P. (1994). *What you can change and what you can't.* New York: Alfred A. Knopf.

Slavin, R. E. (1987). Ability grouping on student achievement in elementary schools: A best evidence synthesis. *Research of Educational Research, 57*, 293–336.

Snowman, J., & McCown, R. (1984, April). *Cognitive processes in learning: A model for investigating strategies and tactics.* Paper presented at the annual meeting of the American Educational Research Association, New Orleans, LA.

Solomon, I. (1995). Analogical transfer and "functional fixedness" in the science classroom. *Journal of Educational Research, 87*(6), 371–377.

Spearitt, D. (1972). Identification of sub-skills of reading comprehension by maximum likelihood factor analysis. *Reading Research Quarterly, 8*, 92–111.

Spiro, R. J., Coulson, R. L., Feltovich, P. J., & Anderson, D. K. (1994). Cognitive flexibility theory: Advanced knowledge acquisition in ill-structured domains. In R. B. Ruddell, M. R. Ruddell, & H Singer (Eds.), *Theoretical models and processes of reading* (4th ed., pp. 602–610). Newark, DE: International Reading Association.

Stahl, S. A., & Fairbanks, M. M. (1986). The effects of vocabulary instruction: A model-based meta-analysis. *Review of Educational Research, 56*(1), 72–110.

Sternberg, R. J. (1977). *Intelligence, information processing and analogical reasoning: The componential analysis of human abilities.* Hillsdale, NJ: Erlbaum.

Sternberg, R. J. (1978). *Toward a unified componential theory of human reasoning* (Tech. Rep. No. 4). New Haven, CT: Yale University, Department of Psychology. (ERIC Document Reproduction Service No. ED 154 421)

Sternberg, R. J. (1979). *The development of human intelligence* (Tech. Rep. No. 4, Cognitive Development Series). New Haven, CT: Yale University, Department of Psychology. (ERIC Document Reproduction Service No. ED 174–658)

Sticht, T. G., Hofstetter, C. R., & Hofsetter, C. H. (1997). *Knowledge, literacy, and power.* San Diego, CA: Consortium for Workforce Education and Lifelong Learning.

Stipek, D. J., & Weisz, J. R. (1981). Perceived personal control and academic achievement. *Review of Educational Research, 51*(1), 101–137.

Stone, C. L. (1983). A meta-analysis of advanced organizer studies. *Journal of Experimental Education, 51*(7), 194–199.

Strang, R. (1975). *Homework: What research says to teachers* (Series). Washington, DC: National Education Association.

Swanborn, M. S. L., & de Glopper, K. (1999). Incidental word learning while reading: A meta-analysis. *Review of Educational Research, 69*(3), 261–285.

Sweitzer, G. L., & Anderson, R. D. (1983). A meta-analysis of research in science teacher education practices associated with inquiry strategy. *Journal of Research in Science Teaching, 20*, 453–466.

Swift, J. N., & Gooding, C. T. (1983). Interaction of wait time feedback and questioning instruction on middle school science teaching. *Journal of Research in Science Teaching, 20*, 721–730.

Taba, H. (1962). *Curriculum development: Theory and practice.* New York: Harcourt, Brace, and World.

Tamir, P. (1985). Meta-analysis of cognitive preferences and learning. *Journal of Research in Science Teaching, 22*(1), 1–17.

Tennebaum, G., & Goldring, E. (1989). A meta-analysis of the effect of enhanced instruction: Cues, participation, reinforcement, and feedback and correctives on motor skill learning. *Journal of Research and Development in Education, 22*(3), 53–64.

Thorndike, R. L. & Lorge, I. (1943). *The teacher's word book of 30,000 words.* New York: Teacher's College Press.

Tobin, K. (1987). The role of wait time in higher cognitive level learning. *Review of Educational Research, 57*, 69–95.

Trammel, D. L., Schloss, P. J., & Alper, S. (1994). Using self-recording and graphing to increase completion of homework assignments. *Journal of Learning Disabilities, 27*(2), 75–81.

Tymms, P. B., & Fitz-Gibbin, C. T. (1992). The relationship of homework to A-level results. *Educational Research, 34*(1), 3–10.

Urdan, T., Midgley, C., & Anderman, E. M. (1998). The role of classroom goal structure in students' use of self-handicapping strategies. *American Educational Research Journal, 35*(1), 101–122.

van Dijk, T. A. (1980). *Macrostructures.* Hillsdale, NJ: Lawrence Erlbaum.

Van Matre, N. H., & Carter, J. F. (1975, March 30–April 4). *The effects of notetaking review on retention of information presented by lecture.* Paper presented at the Annual Meeting of the American Educational Research Association, Washington, DC.

Van Overwalle, F., & De Metsenaere, M. (1990). The effects of attribution-based intervention and study strategy training on academic achievement in college freshmen. *British Journal of Educational Psychology, 60*, 299–311.

Van Secker, C. E., & Lissitz, R. W. (1999). Estimating the impact of instructional practices on student achievement in science. *Journal of Research in Science Teaching 36*(10), 1110–1126.

Vollmer, D. J. (1995). The effects of goal setting on homework behavior, self-efficacy, and attributional aspirations of high school students. *Dissertation Abstracts International, 54*(4–A). (October, 1993, 1298. ISSN 0419–4217)

Walberg, H. J. (1999). Productive teaching. In H. C. Waxman & H. J. Walberg (Eds.) *New directions for teaching practice and research*, 75–104. Berkeley, CA: McCutchen Publishing Corporation.

Wang, M. C., Haertel, G. D., & Walberg, H. J. (1993). Toward a knowledge base for school learning. *Review of Educational Research, 63*(3), 249–294.

Webb, N. M. (1982). Group composition, group interaction, and achievement in cooperative small groups. *Journal of Educational Psychology, 74*, 475–484.

Weiner, B. (1972). Attribution theory, achievement, motivation, and the educational process. *Review of Educational Research, 42*, 203–215.

Weiner, B. (1983). Speculations regarding the role of affect in achievement-change programs guided by attributional principals. In J. M. Levine & M. C. Wang (Eds.), *Teaching and student perceptions: Implications for learning* (pp. 57–73). Hillsdale, NJ: Lawrence Erlbaum.

Welch, M. (1997, April). *Students' use of three-dimensional modeling while designing and making a solution to a technical problem.* Paper presented at the annual meeting of the American Educational Research Association, Chicago.

White, R. T., & Tisher, R. P. (1986). Research on natural sciences. In M. C. Wittrock (Ed.), *Handbook of research on teaching* (pp. 874–905). New York: McMillan.

Wiersma, U. J. C. (1992). The effects of extrinsic reward on intrinsic motivation: A meta-analysis. *Journal of Occupational and Organizational Psychology, 65*, 101–114.

Wiggins, G. (1993). *Assessing student performances: Exploring the purpose and limits of testing.* San Francisco: Jossey-Bass.

Wilburn, K. T., & Felps, B. C. (1983). *Do pupil grading methods affect middle school students' achievement? A comparison of criterion-referenced versus norm-referenced evaluation.* Jacksonville, FL: Wofson Senior High School. (ERIC Document Reproduction Service No. ED 229–451)

Wilkinson, S. S. (1981). The relationship of teacher praise and student achievement: A meta-analysis of selected research. *Dissertation Abstracts International, 41*, 3998A.

Willoughby, T., Desmarias, S., Wood, E., Sims, S., & Kalra, M. (1997). Mechanisms that facilitate the effectiveness of elaboration strategies. *Journal of Educational Psychology, 89*(4), 682–685.

Wilson, T. D., & Linville, P. W. (1982). Improving the academic performance of college freshmen: Attribution theory revisited. *Journal of Personal and Social Psychology, 42*, 367–376.

Wise, K. C., & Okey, J. R. (1983). A meta-analysis of the effects of various science teaching strategies on achievement. *Journal of Research in Science Teaching, 20*(5), 415–425.

Woloshyn, V. E., Willoughby, T., Wood, E., & Pressley, M. (1990). Elaborative interrogation facilitates adult learning of factual paragraphs. *Journal of Educational Psychology, 82*, 513–524.

Wright, S. P., Horn, S. P. &, Sanders, W. L. (1997). Teacher & classroom context effects on student achievement: Implications for teacher evaluation. *Journal of Personnel Evaluation in Education, 11*, 57–67.

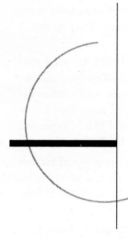

INDEX

Note: Citations to figures are followed by *f*.

ABOUT THE AUTHORS

Robert J. Marzano is a Senior Fellow at Mid-continent Research for Education and Learning (McREL) Institute in Aurora, Colorado. He is responsible for translating research and theory into classroom practice. He headed a team of authors who developed *Dimensions of Learning*, published by the Association for Supervision and Curriculum Development (ASCD), and is also the senior author of *Tactics for Thinking* (ASCD) and *Literacy Plus: An Integrated Approach to Teaching Reading, Writing, Vocabulary, and Reasoning* (Zaner-Bloser). His most recent efforts address standards as described in the two books *Essential Knowledge: The Debate Over What American Students Should Know* (Marzano, Kendall, & Gaddy/McREL, 1999) and *A Comprehensive Guide to Designing Standards-Based Districts, Schools, and Classrooms* (Marzano & Kendall, ASCD/McREL, 1996). He has also recently completed books entitled *Transforming Classroom Grading* (ASCD, 2000) and *Designing a New Taxonomy of Educational Objectives* (Corwin Press, 2000). He has developed programs and practices used in K–12 classrooms that translate current research and theory in cognition into instructional methods.

Marzano received his B.A. in English from Iona College in New York; an M.Ed. in Reading/Language Arts from Seattle University, Seattle, Washington; and a Ph.D. in Curriculum and Instruction from the University of Washington, Seattle. Prior to his work with McREL, Marzano was a tenured associate professor at the University of Colorado at Denver, and a high school English teacher and department chair.

An internationally known trainer and speaker, Marzano has authored 18 books and more than 150 articles and chapters in books on such topics as reading and writing instruction, thinking skills, school effectiveness, restructuring, assessment, cognition, and standards implementation.

He may be contacted at McREL, 2550 S. Parker Rd., Suite 500, Aurora, CO 80014. Phone: 303-632-5534. Fax: 303-337-3005. E-mail: bmarzano@mcrel.org.

Debra J. Pickering is a private consultant and Director of Educational Content for TopTutors.com. During more than 25 years in education, she has gained practical experience as a classroom teacher and district staff development coordinator and has done extensive consulting with administrators and teachers, K–12. Her work in research and development centers on the study of learning and the development of curriculum, instruction and assessment that addresses clearly identified learning goals. With a combination of theoretical grounding and practical experience in the "real world," Pickering works with educators throughout the world who are attempting to translate theory into practice.

Pickering has coauthored a number of articles and programs, including *Dimensions of Learning Teacher's Manual* (2nd ed.) and other materials for ASCD's Dimensions of Learning series, a comprehensive model of learning that provides a framework for developing students who are independent learners and complex thinkers.

She received a B.S. degree in English/Drama Education from the University of Missouri, an M.A. in School Administration from the University of Denver, and a Ph.D. in Curriculum and Instruction with an emphasis on Cognitive Psychology from the University of Denver.

Pickering can be contacted at 10098 East Powers Ave., Englewood, CO 80111. Phone: 303-694-9899. E-mail: djplearn@hotmail.com.

Jane E. Pollock, a researcher and trainer in the areas of standards, assessment, grading and record keeping, curriculum and instruction, and supervision, is a Principal Consultant for the McREL Institute in Aurora, Colorado. She has worked as a classroom teacher, district administrator, university professor, state department staff development coordinator, and K–12 curriculum coordinator.

In consultation with school districts and as part of state initiatives, Pollock designs curriculum based on state and national standards, aligned with state and national assessments. In addition, Pollock works side-by-side with teachers to develop classroom lessons and performance assessments. She organizes various national and international consortiums of schools to help improve student achievement using standards-based programs.

Pollock has conducted workshops in English and in Spanish in the United States, Australia, Canada, and many Central and South American countries. She is coauthor of ASCD's *Dimensions of Learning Teacher's Manual* and *Trainer's Manual* and *Research Into Practice Series on Classroom Instruction* and *Assessment, Grading, and Record Keeping.*

A native of Caracas, Venezuela, Pollock earned a B.A. at Duke University and an M.A. and Ph.D. at the University of Colorado at Boulder. She can be contacted at McREL, 2550 S. Parker Road, Aurora, CO 80014. Phone: 303-632-5508. E-mail: jpollock@mcrel.org.

Related ASCD Resources: Instructional Strategies That Work

ASCD stock numbers are noted in parentheses.

Audiotapes

Instructional Approaches of Superior Teachers (#299202) by Lloyd Campbell

Planning Units Around Essential Understanding & Questions (#298294) by Lynn Erickson

Putting Best Practices to Work on Behalf of Improving Student Learning (#298132) by Kathleen Fitzpatrick

Teaching for the 21st Century (#297247) by Linda Darling-Hammond

Using Dimensions of Learning as a Tool to Increase Student Success (#200120) by James Riedl and Lucinda Riedl

Online Professional Development

Go to ASCD's Home Page (http://www.ascd.org) and click on Training Opportunities:

ASCD Online Tutorials on Standards, Differentiating Instruction, and the Brain and Learning

ASCD Professional Development Online Courses in Differentiating Instruction, Leadership, and the Brain and Learning

Print Products

Becoming a Better Teacher: Eight Innovations That Work (#100043) by Giselle Martin-Kniep

The Differentiated Classroom: Responding to the Needs of All Learners (#199040) by Carol Ann Tomlinson

Dimensions of Learning Teachers' Manual, 2nd Edition (#197133) by Robert J. Marzano, Debra Pickering, and others

Educating Everybody's Children: Diverse Teaching Strategies for Diverse Learners (#195024) edited by Robert Cole

Enhancing Professional Practice: A Framework for Teaching (#196074) by Charlotte Danielson

A Field Guide to Using Visual Tools (#100023) by David Hyerle

A Different Kind of Classroom: Teaching with Dimensions of Learning (#61192107) by Robert J. Marzano

Research You Can Use to Improve Results (#399238) by Kathleen Cotton

Tools for Learning: A Guide for Teaching Study Skills (#61190086) by M. D. Gall, Joyce P. Gall, Dennis R. Jacobsen, and Terry L. Bullock

Understanding by Design (#198199) by Grant Wiggins and Jay McTighe

The Understanding by Design Handbook (#199030) by Jay McTighe and Grant Wiggins

Visual Tools for Constructing Knowledge (#196072) by David Hyerle

Videotapes

Helping Students Acquire and Integrate Knowledge Series (5 videos) (#496065) by Robert Marzano

How to Improve Your Questioning Techniques (#499047), Tape 5 of the "How To" Series

How to Use Graphic Organizers to Promote Student Thinking (#499048), Tape 6 of the "How To" Series

Concept Definition Map (#499262), Tape 5 of The Lesson Collection Video Series: Reading Strategies

Library of Teaching Strategies Part I & II (#614178)

For additional resources, visit us on the World Wide Web (http://www.ascd.org), send an e-mail message to member@ascd.org, call the ASCD Service Center (1-800-933-ASCD or 703-578-9600, then press 2), send a fax to 703-575-5400, or write to Information Services, ASCD, 1703 N. Beauregard St., Alexandria, VA 22311-1714 USA.